AIRCRAFT OF WORLD WAR II

DEVELOPMENT • WEAPONRY • SPECIFICATIONS

AIRCRAFT OF WORLD WAR II

DEVELOPMENT • WEAPONRY • SPECIFICATIONS

Robert Jackson

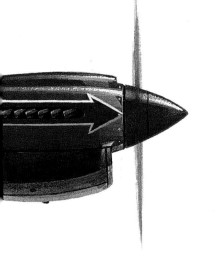

CHARTWELL
BOOKS, INC.

Published by
CHARTWELL BOOKS, INC.
A Division of BOOK SALES, INC.
114 Northfield Avenue
Edison, New Jersey 08837

ISBN 0-7858-1696-8

Editorial and design by
Amber Books Ltd
Bradley's Close
74–77 White Lion Street
London N1 9PF
www.amberbooks.co.uk

Project Editor: James Bennett
Design: Zoe Mellors

Printed in Singapore

Contents

INTRODUCTION

At no other time in history did science and technology make faster progress than in the years between 1939 and 1945, and in no area was progress swifter and more dramatic than in the design of military aircraft, some of them developed in response to requirements that had scarcely been envisaged in the years prior to World War II.

When Britain and France declared war on Germany on 3 September 1939, both countries anticipated massive air attacks from the start of hostilities, but the waves of German bombers never came. It was RAF Bomber Command that struck the first blow, when ten Bristol Blenheim bombers carried out a daylight raid on units of the German fleet in the Elbe estuary on 4 September. No significant damage was caused, and five

The Ju 87 dive-bomber proved highly effective when unopposed in the air.

Blenheims were shot down by flak. Later in the day, the Luftwaffe scored its first victory of the war against the RAF when a Wellington bomber of No 9 Squadron was shot down by a Messerschmitt Bf 109 fighter. In the first weeks of the war RAF bombers, attempting to attack enemy warships in harbour and in daylight, suffered terrible losses, one of the reasons being that the British aircraft were not fitted with self-sealing fuel tanks. Meanwhile, on Germany's western frontier, the initial alarms that had followed the outbreak of hostilities had given way to the uneasy period known as the 'Phoney War'. Only in the air was there any real activity, as British, French and German fighters met in frequent skirmishes over the threatened borders. During these battles the Messerschmitt Bf 109's performance proved superior to that of the Hawker Hurricane, which equipped four RAF squadrons in France, and the French Morane 406 and Curtiss Hawk fighters. It was certainly superior to that of the Gloster Gladiator biplane, which equipped two fighter squadrons assigned to the British Expeditionary Force; yet it was the Gladiator that had to hold the line for the Allies when, on 9 April 1940, the Germans launched an invasion of Norway.

At dawn on 10 May 1940, while the fighting in Norway still raged, the Germans launched their offensive against France, Belgium and Holland, attacking 72 Allied airfields. Within a matter of weeks France had collapsed, and Spitfires, Hurricanes and Messerschmitts were battling for supremacy over the British Isles. During this decisive air battle, weaknesses on both sides were quickly exposed. Not the least of these was that the two most widely used German bombers, the Dornier Do 17 and the Heinkel He 111, lacked adequate defensive armament and could not operate by daylight in a hostile fighter environment, with no fighter escort of their own, without suffering punitive

Luftwaffe mechanics readying a Messerschmitt Bf 109 for action.

losses. That lesson had to be learned and re-learned time and again by the bomber forces of both sides in the course of the war.

To compensate for the Hurricane's inferiority to the Bf 109E, Fighter Command adopted tactics whereby Hurricanes would attack the enemy bombers while Spitfires engaged the German fighter escort. The Spitfire was slightly faster than the Bf 109 and certainly more manoeuvrable, although the Messerschmitt had the edge at high altitude. However, the early attacks on targets in southern England brought a growing confirmation of the Bf 109E's most serious deficiency: a combat radius far shorter than was necessary when escorting bomber formations. During the Battle of France, the Messerschmitt units had been able to provide effective air cover over the rapidly advancing German ground forces only by leapfrogging from one forward airstrip to another, and only a highly efficient Luftwaffe support echelon had kept the fighters in

The He 111 suffered heavy losses in daylight.

action. A greater endurance and range built into the Bf 109E would have eased tremendously the workload imposed on the Luftwaffe logistics system.

As for the twin-engined Messerschmitt Bf 110, intended as a long-range escort fighter, its poor acceleration and wide radius of turn made it no match for the Spitfire, but it was a good 40mph faster than the Hurricane and it carried a formidable armament. If a Bf 110 had an opportunity to make a high-speed attack from high level and break off after a single firing pass, it could be very effective; but such opportunities were rare over England, and the Bf 110 squadrons suffered appalling losses. It was the Bf 109, therefore, that bore the brunt of the escort work, and there can be little doubt that its lack of range was a critical factor in the defeat of the Luftwaffe. The Bf 109E never had more than 20 minutes of combat time in which to protect its bombers, and its combat radius would take it only as far as the northern suburbs of London. Had the 109 been able to extend its time in the combat area by another 30 minutes through the use of external fuel tanks, then the consequences to Fighter Command might have been dire.

The progressive switch of the Luftwaffe to night attacks in the closing weeks of 1940 hastened the development of the dedicated night fighter, the first of which was the Bristol Beaufighter. Supplemented and then eventually replaced by the night fighter variants of the de Havilland Mosquito, the aircraft that really defeated the enemy night bombers, the Beaufighter found a new role as a formidable anti-shipping aircraft, a role also assumed by fighter-bomber Mosquitoes. But it was for its daring low-level attacks on precision targets in occupied Europe that the Mosquito would always be remembered.

In fighter-versus-fighter combat, nowhere was the disparity between aircraft more apparent than on the Russian front. By noon on 22 June 1941, the day the Germans launched their invasion of the Soviet Union, 800 Russian aircraft had been destroyed.

During the latter half of 1941 Russian fighter production concentrated on the more modern types that had begun to replace the elderly I-16s and I-153s: the Yak-1, MiG-1 and LaGG-3.

By the summer of 1942 the Soviet aircraft industry's output was beginning to pick up, and more new fighter types were making their appearance. The first of these was the Lavochkin La-5, which was developed from the LaGG-3. The other fighter aircraft which made its operational debut in 1942 was the Yakovlev Yak-9, a progressive development of the Yak-1.

In the area of ground attack, so vital on the Russian Front, with huge formations of armour constantly in motion, one aircraft in particular shone. Destined to become one of the most famous ground-attack aircraft of all time, the Ilyushin Il-2 suffered serious losses in its early operational career, mainly because it lacked a rear gun position, and although a much modified single-seater with heavier armament, the Il-2M, began to reach front-line units in the autumn of 1942, it was not until August 1943 that a two-seater version made its appearance. This was the Il-2m3, which thereafter played a prominent and often decisive role on the Eastern Front.

As the summer of 1943 turned into autumn, the air war in the west was taking on a new dimension. Bomber Command's night offensive crept inexorably towards the German capital. On the night of 18/19 November, the opening blow was struck in the Battle of Berlin. The offensive was to last until 24 March 1944, during which period 16 major operations were mounted against the city. The assault, which involved the despatch of 9111 bomber sorties, cost the RAF 92 aircraft destroyed over enemy territory and 954 damaged, of which 95 were beyond repair.

For the Americans, August 1943 was a terrible month. It culminated in the 'Anniversary Raids' of 17 August, so called because they marked the anniversary of

A Short Stirling being bombed up.

The Boeing B-17 was the cornerstone of the USAAF's bomber effort in Europe.

the Eighth Air Force's first combat mission over Europe. On this day, 376 B-17s were despatched to attack ball-bearing factories at Schweinfurt and the Messerschmitt assembly plant at Regensburg. The Regensburg force was to fly on to North Africa after bombing. Both targets were hit, but 60 bombers were shot down and many more were badly damaged.

Not until 1944, when North American P-51 Mustang long-range escort fighters became available in numbers, would matters improve; and even then, other dangers were to emerge, the greatest of which was the operational deployment of the world's first jet fighter, the Messerschmitt Me 262. The advent of these formidable aircraft might have proved decisive had they been used in the pure fighter role. Similarly, the Arado Ar 234 jet bomber might have presented insoluble problems to the Allies, had it been available in sufficient numbers earlier in the Battle of Germany.

Following the Allied landings in Normandy on 6 June 1944, the air war in north-west Europe became one of tactical support. The Germans had learned the value of tactical air support in the Spanish Civil War; the RAF's Desert Air Force had developed the concept further in North Africa and subsequently in Italy; and now, in the closing months of the war, it was brought to a fine art by aircraft like the Hawker Typhoon and Republic P-47

Thunderbolt, launching merciless attacks on the retreating Germans.

In the Pacific War, range was the keyword. Since 1940, the Imperial Japanese Navy had been fitting long-range fuel tanks to its excellent Mitsubishi A6M Zero fighters so that they could escort bombers on long-range missions into China, and when Japan went to war in the Pacific its pilots were already highly experienced in flying for range and endurance. The Zero retained its superiority throughout 1942, but in 1943

impressive new Allied combat aircraft began to make their appearance. These were the Vought F4U Corsair, the Lockheed P-38 Lightning and the Grumman F6F Hellcat. The Hellcat, in particular, was able to carry the war to the Japanese home islands.

By July 1945 mastery of the Japanese skies belonged to the Allies, and the Japanese fighters, those that had not been expended in Kamikaze suicide attacks on the Allied fleet, lay immobilized through lack of fuel or pulverized by air attack. When the atomic bombs fell on Hiroshima and Nagasaki, they served merely to underline a victory that had already been won by the relentless application of air and naval might. And the aircraft that dropped the atomic bombs, the mighty Boeing B-29 Superfortress, was the bludgeon that had already destroyed much of Japan's industrial capacity to wage war.

P-47 Thunderbolts make a low pass over a US airfield in the Pacific.

FRANCE

DEWOITINE D.520

*The Dewoitine company was one of the main
suppliers of combat aircraft to the
French Air Force in the
inter-war years, the D.520
being its most modern
design.*

This D.520 is camouflaged
in the standard French Air
Force scheme of May
1940. Aircraft serving with
the Vichy French Air Force at
a later date carried
horizontal red and yellow
identification stripes on the
tail fin, rear fuselage and
nose, forward of the wing
leading edge.

Power for the aircraft was provided by a Hispano-Suiza 12Y-45 12-cylinder Vee-type engine. This was one of France's better aero-engines of the time.

Primary armament of the D.520 was a 20mm (0.79in) Hispano-Suiza cannon mounted between the engine's cylinder banks and firing through the propeller hub.

The D.520's cockpit was set well back in the fuselage, aft of the trailing edge. This gave the pilot good downward visibility, but the extensive nose area in front of him was a drawback when taxiing on the ground.

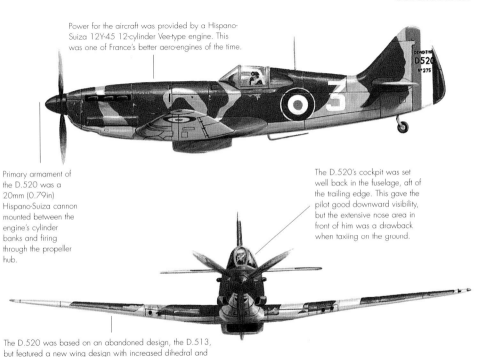

The D.520 was based on an abandoned design, the D.513, but featured a new wing design with increased dihedral and straight-tapered rather than semi-elliptical leading edges.

FRANCE

FRANCE

The D.520 was without doubt the best of France's home-produced fighters at the time of the German invasion in May 1940. It originated as a private venture, design work starting in 1936, and the first prototype flew on 2 October 1938. An initial order for 200 was placed in April 1939, and the eventual total on order up to April 1940

The prototype D.520 shows its paces over southern France in October 1938.

was 2200 for the *Armée de l'Air* and 120 for the *Aeronavale*. When the Germans struck on 10 May 1940 only 36 D.520s had been delivered, and these were operational with GC I/3. Four more *Groupes de Chasse* and three naval *Escadrilles* rearmed with the type before France's surrender, but only GC I/3, II/7, II/6 and the naval AC 1 saw any action. The D.520 *Groupes* claimed 114 victories and 39 probables; 85 D.520s were lost, 165 D.520s were evacuated to North Africa and a further 180 machines were built after the armistice, bringing the production total to 905. The Dewoitine fighter saw limited action against the British and Free French forces in the Syrian campaign of July 1941, and during the Allied invasion of North Africa in November 1942. Some D.520s

Dewoitine D.520

Powerplant:	694kW (930hp) Hispano-Suiza 12Y-45 12-cylinder V-type
Performance:	maximum speed 540km/h (336mph); service ceiling 11,000m (36,090ft); range 1540km (957 miles)
Weights:	empty 2125kg (4685lb); maximum take-off 2790kg (6152lb)
Dimensions:	wing span 10.20m (33ft 5.5in); length 8.76m (28ft 9in); height 2.56m (8ft 5in)
Armament:	one 20mm (0.79in) cannon; four 7.5mm (0.295in) machine guns

served with the Luftwaffe and the air forces of Bulgaria, Romania and Italy after 1942, and with the Free French Air Force in 1944.

The D.520 had exceptionally clean lines, as this view shows.

FRANCE

MORANE-SAULNIER MS.406

*Although manoeuvrable and able to withstand a
great deal of battle damage, the Morane-Saulnier
MS.406 monoplane fighter fared
poorly in combat with the
Messerschmitt Bf 109.*

The pilot was equipped with a simple ring-
and-bead gunsight, mounted outside the
cockpit. The glazed cockpit canopy slid
backwards, and although an attempt had
been made to provide as much glazing as
possible to the rear of the pilot's seat, his
rearward vision was still limited.

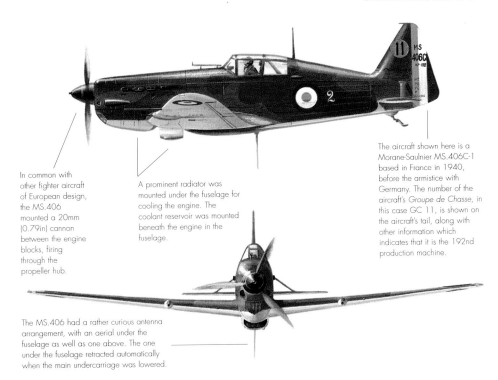

In common with other fighter aircraft of European design, the MS.406 mounted a 20mm (0.79in) cannon between the engine blocks, firing through the propeller hub.

A prominent radiator was mounted under the fuselage for cooling the engine. The coolant reservoir was mounted beneath the engine in the fuselage.

The aircraft shown here is a Morane-Saulnier MS.406C-1 based in France in 1940, before the armistice with Germany. The number of the aircraft's *Groupe de Chasse*, in this case GC 11, is shown on the aircraft's tail, along with other information which indicates that it is the 192nd production machine.

The MS.406 had a rather curious antenna arrangement, with an aerial under the fuselage as well as one above. The one under the fuselage retracted automatically when the main undercarriage was lowered.

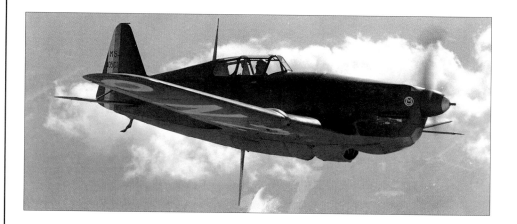

The Morane-Saulnier MS.406 was developed from the MS.405 monoplane fighter, which had a basic all-metal structure, a retractable main undercarriage, and which first flew on 8 August 1935. Early in 1937 the company received an order for 15 pre-production MS.405s, and a slightly different version to

The MS.406 had an unusual folding aerial arrangement below the fuselage.

be designated MS.406. A subsequent order for 50 MS.405s was later changed to cover the same number of MS.406s, so the actual number of MS.405s produced was 17, including the two prototypes.

OUTCLASSED AND OUTFOUGHT

In terms of numbers, the MS.406 was the most important fighter in French service in September 1939. The number eventually built reached 1080, some of which were exported to Switzerland and Turkey. The MS.406 equipped 16 *Groupes de Chasse* and three *Escadrilles* in France and overseas, and 12 of the *Groupes* saw action against the Luftwaffe. The aircraft was very manoeuvrable and could withstand heavy battle damage, but it was outclassed by the Bf 109 and losses were heavy (150 aircraft lost in action and 250–300 lost through other causes). After the armistice only one

Morane-Saulnier MS.406

Powerplant:	641kW (860hp) Hispano-Suiza 12Y-31 12-cylinder V-type
Performance:	maximum speed 490km/h (304mph); service ceiling 9400m (30,850ft); range 1500km (932 miles)
Weights:	empty 1872kg (4127lb); maximum take-off 2722kg (6000lb) Dimensions: wing span 10.62m (34ft 5in); length 8.17m (26ft 9in); height 3.25m (10ft 8in)
Armament:	one 20mm (0.79in) cannon or 7.5mm (0.295in) machine gun and two 7.5mm machine guns

Vichy unit, GC I/7, was equipped with the MS.406. Some captured aircraft were handed over to Finland and Croatia.

The pilot of an MS.406 prototype runs up the engine prior to a test flight.

FRANCE

21

ARADO AR 196A-5

This Ar 196A-5 served in the eastern Mediterranean and Aegean with 2/SAGr 125 (Maritime Recce Group 125) in 1943. The units also used Bv 138 flying boats.

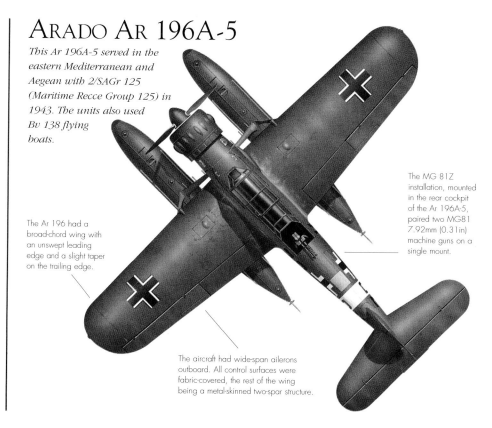

The MG 81Z installation, mounted in the rear cockpit of the Ar 196A-5, paired two MG81 7.92mm (0.31in) machine guns on a single mount.

The Ar 196 had a broad-chord wing with an unswept leading edge and a slight taper on the trailing edge.

The aircraft had wide-span ailerons outboard. All control surfaces were fabric-covered, the rest of the wing being a metal-skinned two-spar structure.

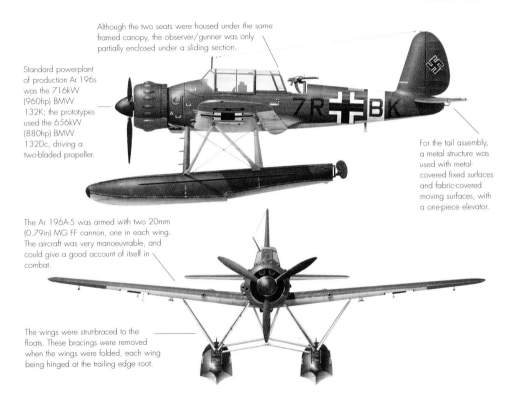

Although the two seats were housed under the same framed canopy, the observer/gunner was only partially enclosed under a sliding section.

Standard powerplant of production Ar 196s was the 716kW (960hp) BMW 132K; the prototypes used the 656kW (880hp) BMW 132Dc, driving a two-bladed propeller.

For the tail assembly, a metal structure was used with metal-covered fixed surfaces and fabric-covered moving surfaces, with a one-piece elevator.

The Ar 196A-5 was armed with two 20mm (0.79in) MG FF cannon, one in each wing. The aircraft was very manoeuvrable, and could give a good account of itself in combat.

The wings were strut-braced to the floats. These bracings were removed when the wings were folded, each wing being hinged at the trailing edge root.

GERMANY

23

GERMANY

The Arado Ar 196A-5 was one of three operational versions of the Ar 196, the others being the Ar 196A-1 and the Ar 196A-3. The aircraft was designed to replace the Heinkel He 50, a catapult-launched biplane carried by major warships in the 1930s. The prototype Ar 196V-1 flew in the summer of 1938 and was followed by

An Arado Ar 196 about to be catapulted from the *Prinz Eugen* during trials.

the Ar 196V-2, both fitted with twin floats; two others, the Ar 196V-3 and V-4, were equipped with a large central float and two stabilizing floats. The latter were prototypes for the Ar 196B, which was later abandoned.

SHIP-BASED OPERATIONS

A pre-production batch of 10 Ar 196A-0 aircraft was followed by 20 production Ar 196A-1s, which operated from Germany's capital ships. The major production model was the Ar 196A-3, which saw extensive service in all theatres. On 5 May 1940 two of these achieved fame by accepting the surrender of HM submarine *Seal*, which had been forced to the surface with mine damage in the Kattegat. Production of the Ar 196, all variants, was 536, including 69 Ar 196A-5s built by Fokker in the Netherlands in 1943–44.

Arado Ar 196 A-5

Powerplant:	723kW (970hp) BMW 132K 9-cylinder radial
Performance:	max speed 320km/h (199mph) at 4000m (13,125ft); service ceiling 7000m (22,960ft); range 1070km (665 miles)
Weights:	empty 2335kg (5148lb); maximum take-off 3303kg (7282lb)
Dimensions:	wing span 12.40m (40ft 8.25in); length 11.00m (36ft 1in); height 4.45m (14ft 7in)
Armament:	two 20mm (0.79in) cannon; one 7.92mm (0.31in) machine gun and two 7.92mm machine guns, plus external bomb load of 100kg (220lb)

The Arado Ar 196 carried a heavy armament and could be a formidable opponent in combat.

GERMANY

25

ARADO AR 234B-2

Able to carry a bomb load of 2000kg (4410lb),
the Arado 234B-2 went
into service with KG 76
in October 1944. Based
at Achmer and Rheine,
the jet bombers made many
successful attacks.

The Ar 234's cockpit was
fitted with an ejection seat
and was pressurized. The
Germans pioneered the
operational use of ejection
seats in their high-speed
aircraft.

The Ar 234B-2 had a slightly
wider fuselage than the
prototypes in order to
accommodate the main
undercarriage units.

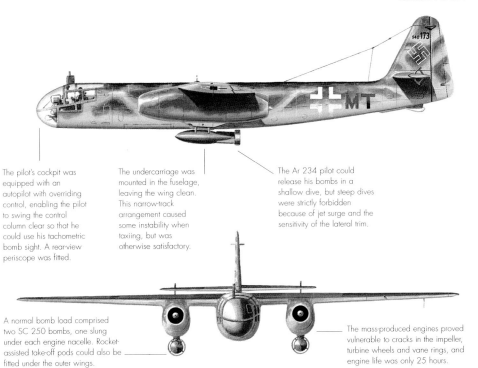

The pilot's cockpit was equipped with an autopilot with overriding control, enabling the pilot to swing the control column clear so that he could use his tachometric bomb sight. A rear-view periscope was fitted.

The undercarriage was mounted in the fuselage, leaving the wing clean. This narrow-track arrangement caused some instability when taxiing, but was otherwise satisfactory.

The Ar 234 pilot could release his bombs in a shallow dive, but steep dives were strictly forbidden because of jet surge and the sensitivity of the lateral trim.

A normal bomb load comprised two SC 250 bombs, one slung under each engine nacelle. Rocket-assisted take-off pods could also be fitted under the outer wings.

The mass-produced engines proved vulnerable to cracks in the impeller, turbine wheels and vane rings, and engine life was only 25 hours.

GERMANY

27

The Arado 234B-2 was the world's first jet bomber, and followed the unarmed Ar 234B-1 reconnaissance version into service. The prototype Ar 234V-1, which flew for the first time on 15 June 1943, and the next seven aircraft used a trolley for take-off and a skid for landing, but this was soon replaced by a

The Ar 234's robust undercarriage was designed for poorly prepared strips.

conventional undercarriage. The first operational sorties (in the reconnaissance role) were flown by the V-5 and V-7 prototypes, which were delivered to *I/Versuchsverband.Ob.d.L* (Luftwaffe High

Command Trials Unit) at Juvincourt, Reims, in July 1944.

ARDENNES OFFENSIVE

The Ar 234B-2 flew its first combat missions with KG 76 during the German offensive in the Ardennes in December 1944. The jet bombers were extremely active in the early weeks of 1945, one of their most notable missions being a ten-day series of attacks on the Ludendorff Bridge at Remagen. Numerous variants were planned, including a four-engined version, the Ar 234C, but only 19 of these had been completed when the war ended. The Ar 234C-3N was a proposed night-fighter variant with two 30mm

Arado Ar 234B-2

Powerplant:	two 800kg (1764lb) thrust BMW 003A-1 turbojets
Performance:	maximum speed 742km/h (461mph) at 6000m (19,685ft); service ceiling 10,000m (32,810ft); range 1630km (1013 miles)
Weights:	empty 5200kg (11,466lb); 9850kg (21,715lb) loaded
Dimensions:	wing span: 14.11m (46ft 3.5in); length 12.64m (41ft 5.5in); height: 4.30m (14ft 1.25in)
Armament:	two 20mm (0.79in) cannon; external bomb load of 1500kg (3307lb)

(1.19in) and two 20mm (0.79in) cannon as well as FuG 218 Neptun AI radar.

The more powerful Ar 234C variant was fitted with four BMW 004B turbojets.

DORNIER DO 17P

Popularly known as the 'Flying Pencil' because of its long, slim fuselage, the Dornier Do 17 was widely used in bomber and reconnaissance roles in the early part of the war.

The original civil version of the Do 17 featured a single fin and rudder. Three aircraft were built with this configuration before twin fins were adopted for the military variant. _____

The Do 17's defensive armament was poor, and was upgraded as a result of losses suffered in the Battle of Britain.

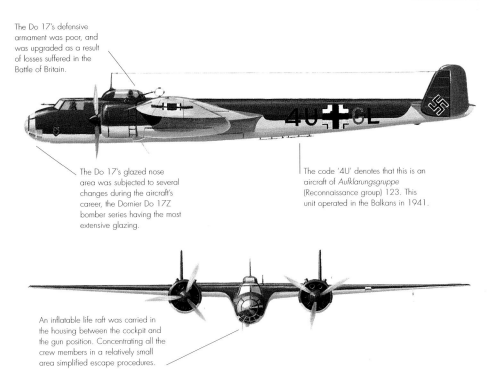

The Do 17's glazed nose area was subjected to several changes during the aircraft's career, the Dornier Do 17Z bomber series having the most extensive glazing.

The code '4U' denotes that this is an aircraft of *Aufklarungsgruppe* (Reconnaissance group) 123. This unit operated in the Balkans in 1941.

An inflatable life raft was carried in the housing between the cockpit and the gun position. Concentrating all the crew members in a relatively small area simplified escape procedures.

The Dornier Do 17P was a photographic reconnaissance version of the famous German bomber, which was originally intended as a fast mailplane for Deutsche Lufthansa but never used in that capacity. The first of 12 prototypes flew in 1934 and the first military examples, the Do 17E-1 and Do 17F-1, entered service in

A Do 17 over the Aegean. The aircraft was widely used in the Greek campaign.

1939. These were intended for the high-speed bomber and long-range reconnaissance roles respectively, the latter having extra fuel tankage and two bomb-bay cameras. The aircraft were powered by two BMW VI 12-cylinder V-type engines and were evaluated in combat during the Spanish Civil War. Development of the Do 17E/F led to the Do 17M/P types, with Bramo 323 radial engines. These were followed by 18 Do 17S/U pre-production types, which preceded the introduction of the definitive radial-engined variant, the Do 17Z, over 500 of which were built. Although faster than most contemporary fighters when it entered service, the Do 17 quickly became obsolescent and suffered heavily in the battles of France and Britain.

Dornier Do 17P

Powerplant:	two 746kW (1000hp) BMW Bramo 323P Fafnir 9-cylinder radials
Performance:	maximum speed 410km/h (255mph) at 1220m (4000ft); service ceiling 8200m (26,900ft); range 1500km (932 miles)
Weights:	empty 5210kg (11,488lb) maximum take-off 8590kg (18,937lb)
Dimensions:	wing span 18m (59ft); length 15.80m (51ft 10in); height 4.60m (15ft 1in)
Armament:	one or two 7.92mm (0.31in) machine guns plus internal bomb load of 1000kg (2205lb)

Seen in the winter of 1941–42, a Do 17 of 7. Staffel III/KG 3 is bombed up. The unit converted to the Ju 88 in 1942.

GERMANY

FOCKE-WULF FW 190A

Known as the 'Butcher Bird' to many of its opponents, the Focke-Wulf Fw 190 made its appearance in the autumn of 1941, and for months established air superiority for the Luftwaffe.

As built, early production Fw 190s were armed with four Rheinmetall Borsig MG.17 machine guns mounted in the upper fuselage and wing roots and firing through the propeller arc. This proved inadequate, and some aircraft were retrofitted with an MGFF cannon in each outer wing.

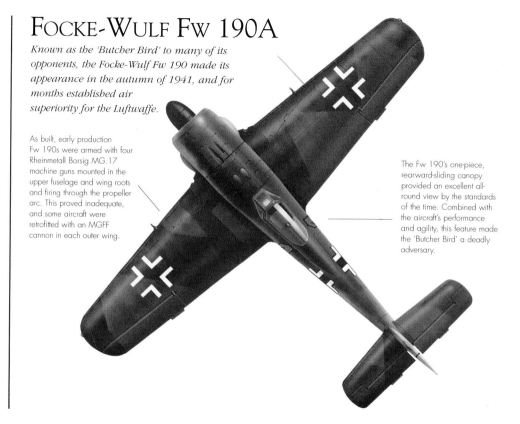

The Fw 190's one-piece, rearward-sliding canopy provided an excellent all-round view by the standards of the time. Combined with the aircraft's performance and agility, this feature made the 'Butcher Bird' a deadly adversary.

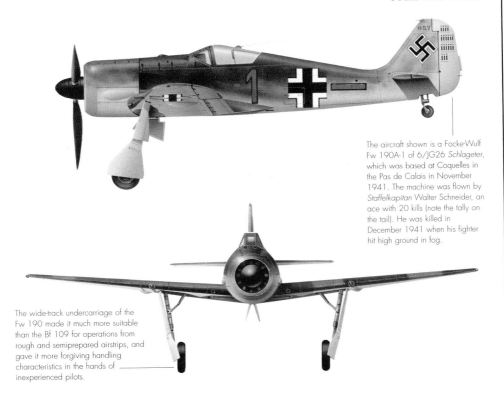

The aircraft shown is a Focke-Wulf Fw 190A-1 of 6/JG26 *Schlageter*, which was based at Coquelles in the Pas de Calais in November 1941. The machine was flown by *Staffelkapitän* Walter Schneider, an ace with 20 kills (note the tally on the tail). He was killed in December 1941 when his fighter hit high ground in fog.

The wide-track undercarriage of the Fw 190 made it much more suitable than the Bf 109 for operations from rough and semiprepared airstrips, and gave it more forgiving handling characteristics in the hands of inexperienced pilots.

GERMANY

The Focke-Wulf Fw 190 started life as an interim fighter, intended to complement the Messerschmitt Bf 109. The first production variant, the Fw 190A-1, went into service with JG26 at Le Bourget, Paris, in August 1941. This was followed into production by the A-2, with a longer span and heavier armament, and the

Factory-fresh Focke-Wulf Fw 190A-5s being collected for delivery to the front.

A-3 fighter-bomber. The next variant, the Fw 190A-4, had a methanol-water power boost system. The A-5, a development of the A-4 with the engine relocated 0.15m (5.9in) farther forward, undertook a variety of roles including ground attack, night fighter, torpedo-bomber and bomber-destroyer. Some A-5s were modified as two-seat Fw 190S-5 trainers. The Fw 190A-6 had a lighter wing structure and an armament of four 20mm (0.79in) cannon, and spawned a number of variants including bomber-destroyers, with 30mm (1.19in) cannon and extra armour to protect the pilot against head-on attacks.

The Fw 190A-7, which entered production in December 1943, had a revised armament of two 20mm cannon in the wing roots and two 12.7mm (0.50in) machine guns in the forward fuselage. It was soon supplanted by the Fw 190A-8, the last new-build variant of the Fw 190A series. Total production of the Fw190

Focke-Wulf Fw 190A-8

Powerplant:	1566kW (2100hp) BMW 801D-2 radial engine
Performance:	maximum speed 654km/h (406mph) at 6000m (19,685ft); service ceiling 11,400m (37,401ft); range 1470km (915 miles)
Weights:	empty 3170kg (7000lb); maximum take-off 4900kg (10,805lb)
Dimensions:	wing span 10.50m (34ft 5.5in); length 8.84m (29ft); height 3.96m (13ft)
Armament:	two 7.92mm (0.31in) machine guns and up to four 20mm (0.79in) cannon in wings, plus provision for under-fuselage and underwing bombs and rockets

(all variants, excluding prototypes) was 20,051 aircraft.

The 'long-nose' Fw 190D-9 variant.

GERMANY

37

FOCKE-WULF FW 200 CONDOR

*In the early years of World War II, the long-range
Focke-Wulf Condor was a far greater threat to
Allied shipping than the German U-boats,
which were not yet
fully deployed.*

The forward-firing 7.92mm
(0.31in) MG 15 machine gun
in the fully enclosed forward
cupola was manned by the
co-pilot when the aircraft was
threatened by frontal attack.

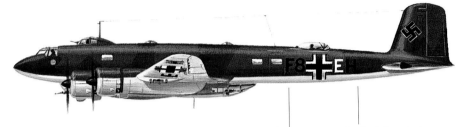

This Condor bears the code markings of KG 40, the Luftwaffe's highly experienced anti-shipping unit. Operating from bases in the Biscay area, KG 40's aircraft ranged as far afield as Norway, their route taking them over the Atlantic to the west of Ireland.

The Condor's rear fuselage was used as a storage area for small stores like flares, light buoys or direction-finding buoys. These were dropped through a hatch in the fuselage underside.

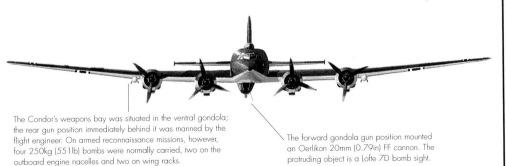

The Condor's weapons bay was situated in the ventral gondola; the rear gun position immediately behind it was manned by the flight engineer. On armed reconnaissance missions, however, four 250kg (551lb) bombs were normally carried, two on the outboard engine nacelles and two on wing racks.

The forward gondola gun position mounted an Oerlikon 20mm (0.79in) FF cannon. The protruding object is a Lofte 7D bomb sight.

GERMANY

39

GERMANY

Originally developed to meet an unfulfilled Japanese requirement, the Focke-Wulf Fw 200 Condor was a maritime bomber/reconnaissance version of the pre-war civil airliner, production of which was taken over by the Luftwaffe. The first unit to receive the production Fw 200C-1 was the Luftwaffe's

Developed from an airliner, the Condor had exceptional range, and was capable of flying from Cherbourg to Norway.

Long-Range Reconnaissance Squadron (*Fernaufklarungsstaffel*), which began operations in April 1940 and was redesignated I/KG 40 later in the month.

The next variant, the Fw 200C-2, differed from the C-1 in having two bomb racks of improved design under each wing. A structurally strengthened version, the Fw 200C-3, was placed in production by mid-1941, and this variant of the Condor was produced in greater numbers than its predecessors.

AIR-TO-SURFACE MISSILE

The final operational version of the Condor was the Fw 200C-6, developed from the C-3 to carry a Henschel Hs 293B air-to-surface missile under each outer engine nacelle, the underwing bomb racks being removed. The combination of Hs 293 and Fw 200 was first used operationally on 28 December 1943. The total number of Condors produced during the war years was 252 aircraft. Many were relegated to transport duties in 1942, nine being lost in attempts to resupply the German garrison at Stalingrad.

Focke-Wulf Fw 200C-3

Powerplant:	four 895kW (1200hp) BMW-Bramo 323R-2 Fafnir nine-cylinder radial engines (FW 200C-3/U4)
Performance:	maximum speed 360km/h (224mph) at 4700m (15,420ft); Service ceiling: 6000m (19,685ft); range: 4440km (2759 miles)
Weights:	empty 17,005kg (37,496lb); maximum take-off 22,700kg (50,044lb)
Dimensions:	wing span 32.84m (107ft 8in); length 23.85m (78ft 3in); height: 6.30m (20ft 8in)
Armament:	two 7.92mm (0.31in) machine guns, three 12.7mm (0.50in) machine guns and one 20mm (0.79in) machine gun, plus a maximum internal and external bomb load of 2100kg (4630lb)

GERMANY

HEINKEL HE 111H

Having first seen service in the Spanish Civil War, the He 111 became the Luftwaffe's most well-known medium bomber.

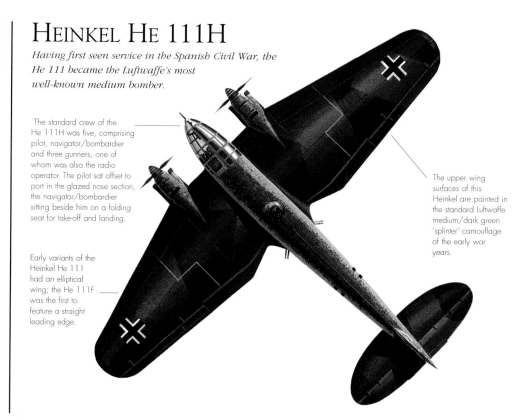

The standard crew of the He 111H was five, comprising pilot, navigator/bombardier and three gunners, one of whom was also the radio operator. The pilot sat offset to port in the glazed nose section, the navigator/bombardier sitting beside him on a folding seat for take-off and landing.

The upper wing surfaces of this Heinkel are painted in the standard Luftwaffe medium/dark green 'splinter' camouflage of the early war years.

Early variants of the Heinkel He 111 had an elliptical wing; the He 111F was the first to feature a straight leading edge.

During the bomb run, the navigator lay on a pad in the extreme nose, on which he lay prone to use the bombsight. He also operated the nose gun, an MGFF 20mm (0.79in) cannon with 180 rounds of ammunition.

The He 111P version, which was powered by two 858kW (1150hp) Daimler-Benz DB 601Aa engines, introduced a fully-glazed asymmetric nose, with its offset ball turret, in place of the stepped-up cockpits of the earlier variants.

The Heinkel He 111 was designed early in 1934 as a high-speed transport and as a bomber for the clandestine new Luftwaffe. The first of several prototypes flew for the first time on 24 February 1935. The aircraft was ordered into production for the Luftwaffe as the He 111B-1, and in 1937 the variant

An He 111H of the Norway-based KG 26 'Lion' *Geschwader* **prior to a sortie.**

was tested under combat conditions with the Condor Legion in Spain. The He 111E and He 111F were powered by Junkers Jumo engines, the latter being the first to feature a wing with a straight leading edge.

BOMBER BACKBONE

In mid-1939 a new model made its appearance. This was the He 111P, which was powered by two 857kW (1150hp) Daimler-Benz DB 601Aa engines and which incorporated a fully-glazed asymmetric nose with an offset ball turret. Relatively few He 111Ps were completed before production switched to the He 111H, the variant which formed the backbone of the Luftwaffe's bomber force between 1940 and 1943, about 6150 being built before production ended in 1944. The final variant of the Heinkel bomber was the He 111Z, which was built to tow the massive Me 321 Gigant glider.

Heinkel He 111H-6

Powerplant:	two 1007kW (1350hp) Junkers Jumo 211F inverted V-12 engines
Performance:	maximum speed 436km/h (271mph) at 6000m (19,685ft); service ceiling 6700m (21,980ft); range 1950km (1212 miles)
Weights:	empty 8680kg (19,139lb); maximum take-off 14,000kg (30,865lb)
Dimensions:	wing span 22.60m (74ft 1.33in); length 16.40m (53ft 9.5in); height 3.40m (11ft 1.5in)
Armament:	one 20mm (0.79in) cannon, one 13mm (0.51in) machine gun and four 7.92mm (0.31in) machine guns plus a maximum bomb load of 4000kg (8818lb)

He 111 bombers over the English Channel during the Battle of Britain.

GERMANY

HENSCHEL HS 123

By the end of World War I, the Germans had amassed considerable experience in the design of close-support aircraft. With a new war approaching, tactical air power was again vital.

This Hs 123A-1 served with *Schlachtgeschwader* 2 on the Eastern Front in the winter of 1942–43. It is fitted with an auxiliary fuel tank, and the wheel spats – an encumbrance when operating from muddy airstrips – have been removed.

The Hs 123 was never given an enclosed cockpit, so conditions for its pilots on the Russian Front in winter were not exactly comfortable – although the heat generated by the big radial helped somewhat.

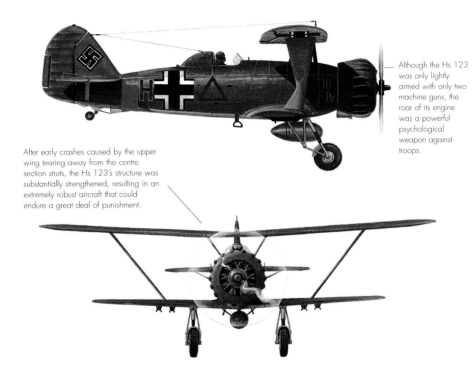

Although the Hs 123 was only lightly armed with only two machine guns, the roar of its engine was a powerful psychological weapon against troops.

After early crashes caused by the upper wing tearing away from the centre section struts, the Hs 123's structure was substantially strengthened, resulting in an extremely robust aircraft that could endure a great deal of punishment.

GERMANY

The Henschel Hs 123 was the Luftwaffe's last operational biplane. It originated in a 1933 specification for a dive-bomber, devised by Ernst Udet, the WWI air ace who was now charged with rebuilding Germany's air arm. The first prototype Hs 123V-1 flew for the first time in May 1935 and the test programme was

Outmoded at the outbreak of war, the Hs 123 was still highly effective.

hit by early tragedy, two of the prototypes shedding their wings during dives. Investigations revealed that the wing had torn away from the centre-section struts, and so the fourth aircraft was substantially strengthened. The type was ordered into production, five Hs 123As being sent to Spain for operational evaluation with the Condor Legion in 1936. This resulted in the improved Hs 123B, which was dedicated to ground attack (rather than dive-bombing) and saw combat during the German invasions of Poland, France and the USSR. Although the Hs 123 carried comparatively light armament, its BMW radial engine was very noisy, especially in a dive, and this was used as a device to spread panic among horses and men alike. Although the Hs 123

Henschel Hs 123A

Powerplant:	656kW (880hp) BMW 132Dc radial
Performance:	maximum speed 340km/h (211mph) at 2000m (6562ft); service ceiling 9000m (29,530ft); range 855km (531 miles)
Weights:	empty 1500kg (3308lb); maximum take-off 2215kg (4883lb)
Dimensions:	wing span 10.50m (34ft 5.5in) upper wing; length 8.33m (27ft 4in); height 3.20m (10ft 6in)
Armament:	two 7.92mm (0.31in) MG17 machine guns; up to 450kg (992lb) of bombs

was obsolescent, one unit, II/SG2, continued to use it on the Russian Front until 1944. The Hs 123C was a variant armed with 20mm (0.79in) cannon.

An Hs 123 used on the Eastern Front in 1942.

GERMANY

49

JUNKERS JU 87 STUKA

Although the word Stuka – *an abbreviation of* Sturzkampfflugzeug – *was applied to all German bomber aircraft with a dive-bombing capability during World War II, it will forever be associated with the Junkers Ju 87.*

The Ju 87's pilot sat under a sliding canopy, surrounded by substantial armour protection. The aircraft had an automatic dive control that would pull it out of its dive at a preset altitude when engaged by the pilot. The pilot operated the two forward-firing Rheinmetall-Borsig 7.92mm (0.31in) MG 17 machine guns, which had 1000 rounds of ammunition each.

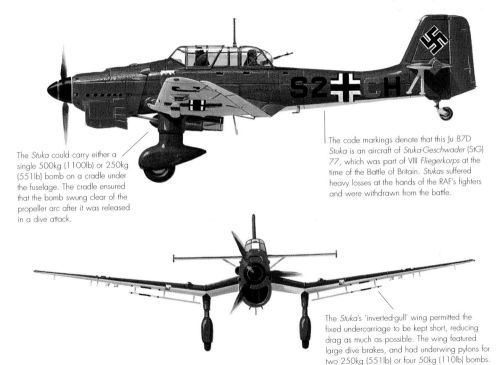

The *Stuka* could carry either a single 500kg (1100lb) or 250kg (551lb) bomb on a cradle under the fuselage. The cradle ensured that the bomb swung clear of the propeller arc after it was released in a dive attack.

The code markings denote that this Ju 87D *Stuka* is an aircraft of *Stuka-Geschwader* (StG) 77, which was part of VIII *Fliegerkorps* at the time of the Battle of Britain. *Stukas* suffered heavy losses at the hands of the RAF's fighters and were withdrawn from the battle.

The *Stuka*'s 'inverted-gull' wing permitted the fixed undercarriage to be kept short, reducing drag as much as possible. The wing featured large dive brakes, and had underwing pylons for two 250kg (551lb) or four 50kg (110lb) bombs.

GERMANY

51

The first prototype Ju 87V-1 flew for the first time in the late spring of 1935, powered by a 477kW (640hp) Rolls-Royce Kestrel engine. This aircraft had twin fins and rudders, replaced by a single fin and rudder in the Ju 87V-2. Deliveries of production aircraft began in 1937. In 1938 an extensively modified version appeared,

A Ju 87B pictured in Greece during the campaign of April–May 1941.

the Ju 87B, which used the more powerful 820kW (1100hp) Jumo 211Da. The aircraft had a redesigned cockpit and a 'spatted' undercarriage. An anti-shipping version of the Ju 87B-2 was known as the Ju 87R.

SHIPBOARD DIVE-BOMBER

The next production model was the Ju 87D, fitted with a 1044kW (1400hp) Jumo 211J-1 with induction cooling. Several sub-series of the Ju 87D were produced in quantity, incorporating modifications for a variety of tasks. The last variant was the anti-tank Ju 87G, a standard Ju 87D-5 converted to carry two BK 37 cannon under the wing. One of the more interesting and little-known versions of the *Stuka* was the Ju 87C, a shipboard dive-bomber intended for service on Germany's planned aircraft carrier, the *Graf Zeppelin*. It had hydraulically operated

Junkers Ju 87D-1

Powerplant: 1044kW (1400hp) Junkers Jumo 211J inverted-Vee piston engine

Performance: maximum speed 410km/h (255mph) at 3840m (12,600ft); service ceiling 7300m (23,950ft); range 1535km (954 miles)

Weights: empty 3900kg (8600lb); maximum take-off 6600kg (14,550lb)

Dimensions: wing span 13.80m (45ft 3.33in); length 11.50m (37ft 8.33in); height 3.88m (12ft 8.75in)

Armament: three 7.92mm (0.31in) machine guns, plus external bomb load of up to 1800kg (3968lb)

folding wings, deck arrester gear and a jettisonable undercarriage.

The yellow fuselage bands indicate that these Ju 87Bs served in the Balkans.

GERMANY

JUNKERS JU 88

*One of the most versatile and effective combat
aircraft ever produced, the Junkers Ju 88
remained of vital importance to the
Luftwaffe throughout World War II,
serving in numerous combat roles.*

The bombardier had easy
access to the glazed nose
section, where a bombsight
was located for conventional
bombing. For dive-bombing,
the pilot used a sight
mounted in the cockpit,
which swung to the side
when not in use.

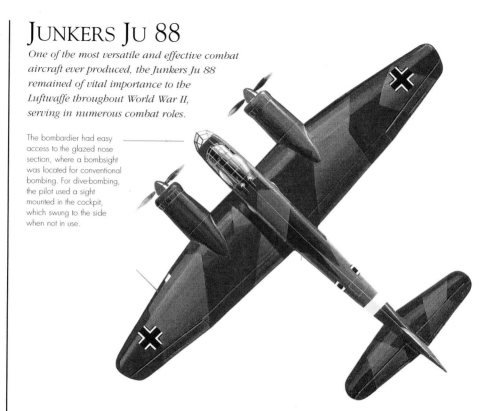

The pilot sat in the front of the glazed cockpit, offset to port, with the navigator/bombardier seated on his right and slightly below him.

The flight engineer had the secondary task of operating the rearward-firing 7.92mm (0.31in) MG 15 machine gun in the rear of the glazed cabin.

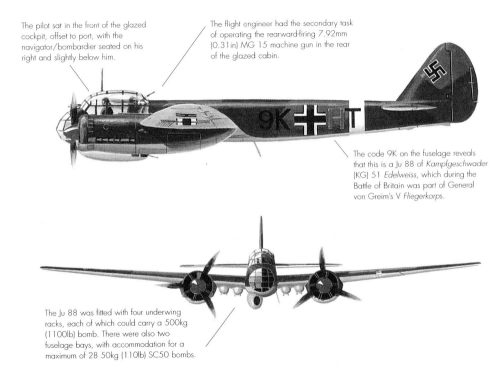

The code 9K on the fuselage reveals that this is a Ju 88 of *Kampfgeschwader* (KG) 51 *Edelweiss*, which during the Battle of Britain was part of General von Greim's V *Fliegerkorps*.

The Ju 88 was fitted with four underwing racks, each of which could carry a 500kg (1100lb) bomb. There were also two fuselage bays, with accommodation for a maximum of 28 50kg (110lb) SC50 bombs.

The prototype Ju 88 flew for the first time on 21 December 1936 and the first pre-series Ju 88A-0s were delivered to the Luftwaffe in August 1939. The Ju 88A was built in 17 different variants up to the Ju 88A-17, with progressively uprated engines and enhanced defensive armament. The most widely used variant

A Ju 88A-5 running up its engines prior to a sortie on the Russian front in 1941.

was the Ju 88A-4, which served in both Europe and North Africa. The Ju 88A saw considerable action in the Balkans and the Mediterranean, and on the Eastern Front. Some of their most outstanding service, however, was in the Arctic, where aircraft of KG 26 and KG 30, based in northern Norway, carried out devastating attacks on Allied convoys to Russia.

FIGHTER VERSIONS

The heavy fighter version of the Ju 88 was the Ju 88C. The Ju 88C-6, and the last variant in this series, the C-7, were used as both day and night fighters. The last fighter variant, which made its appearance in the spring of 1944, was the Ju 88G night fighter. Total Junkers 88 production was 14,676 aircraft, of which about 3900 were fighter or ground-attack variants.

Junkers Ju 88A-1

Powerplant:	two 999kW (1340hp) Junkers Jumo 211J inverted V-12 engines
Performance:	maximum speed 450km/h (280mph) at 6000m (19,685ft); service ceiling 8200m (26,900ft); range 2730km (1696 miles)
Weights:	empty 9860kg (21,741lb); maximum take-off 14,000kg (30,865lb)
Dimensions:	wing span 20.00m (65ft 7.5in); length 14.40m (47ft 3in); height 4.85m (15ft 11in)
Armament:	up to seven 7.92m (0.31in) machine guns, plus a maximum internal and external bomb load of 3600kg (7935lb)

A dramatic shot of Ju 88s in formation. The Ju 88 was one of the best and most versatile bombers of the war.

GERMANY

MESSERSCHMITT BF 109E-4

The Messerschmitt Bf 109, one of the most famous fighters of all time, was the mainstay of the Luftwaffe fighter squadrons for much of the war, and a formidable opponent.

The E-4 differed from the more numerous E-3 in having an improved MG FF/M cannon with an increased rate of fire, but otherwise the armament was identical; the two 20mm (0.79in) cannon were mounted in the wing and a pair of MG 17 machine guns were mounted in the upper forward fuselage.

This Bf 109E bears a standard early-war scheme of dark grey and dark green upper surfaces over light blue fuselage and underside, with white rudder and engine cowling.

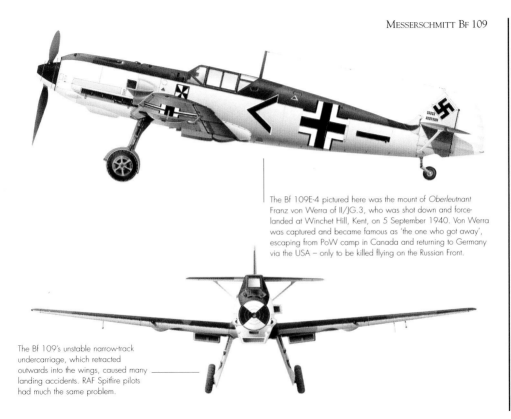

The Bf 109E-4 pictured here was the mount of *Oberleutnant* Franz von Werra of II/JG.3, who was shot down and force-landed at Winchet Hill, Kent, on 5 September 1940. Von Werra was captured and became famous as 'the one who got away', escaping from PoW camp in Canada and returning to Germany via the USA – only to be killed flying on the Russian Front.

The Bf 109's unstable narrow-track undercarriage, which retracted outwards into the wings, caused many landing accidents. RAF Spitfire pilots had much the same problem.

The prototype Bf 109V-1 flew for the first time in September 1935, powered by a 518kW (695hp) Rolls-Royce Kestrel engine, as the 455kW (610hp) Junkers Jumo 210A which was intended for it was not yet available; three subsequent prototypes were evaluated in Spain. The first series production model was

Messerschmitt Bf 109Es of JG 27 over the North African desert in 1942.

the Bf 109B, powered by a 455kW (610hp) Jumo 210 engine. By the outbreak of WWII 1,060 Bf 109s of various sub-species were in service with the Luftwaffe's fighter units. These included the Bf 109C and Bf 109D, which were already being replaced by the Bf 109E series; this model was to be the mainstay of the Luftwaffe's fighter units throughout 1940. The best of all Bf 109 variants, the Bf 109F, began to reach Luftwaffe units in France in May 1941 and was superior in most respects to the principal RAF fighter of the time, the Spitfire Mk V. The Bf 109F differed from the Bf 109E in having a cleaned-up airframe, redesigned engine cowling, wing, radiators and tail assembly. It was succeeded by the Bf 109G, which appeared late in 1942. The Bf 109G was built in Spain as the Hispano Ha 1109 and in Czechoslovakia as the Avia

Messerschmitt Bf 109E-4

Powerplant:	761kW (1020hp) Daimler-Benz DB 601Aa 12-cylinder inverted-Vee engine
Performance:	maximum speed 575km/h (357mph) at 3200m (10,498ft); service ceiling 10,500m (34,448ft); range 660km (410 miles)
Weights:	empty 2125kg (4685lb); maximum take-off 2665kg (5875lb)
Dimensions:	wing span 9.87m (32ft 4.5in); length 8.64m (28ft 4.5in); height 2.50m (8ft 2.5in)
Armament:	two 20mm (0.79in) cannon and two 7.92mm (0.31in) machine guns

S-199. In all, Bf 109 production reached a total of about 35,000 aircraft.

Messerschmitt Bf 109G 'Black Six' before the 1997 crash which ended her flying days.

GERMANY

MESSERSCHMITT BF 110G

The Messerschmitt Bf 110 was a failure in its intended role as a long-range escort fighter, but went on to prove its worth as a night fighter, scoring many successes against the RAF's night bombers.

The Bf 110 was designed to carry a crew of three, comprising pilot, radio operator and gunner. In practice a crew of two was usually carried, the radio operator also acting as the gunner. The Bf 110C-4 was the first variant to introduce armour protection for the crew.

The gunner was armed with a single 7.92mm (0.31in) MG 15 machine gun with 750 rounds of ammunition. The hood on his section of the cockpit could be swung upwards to give a better field of fire.

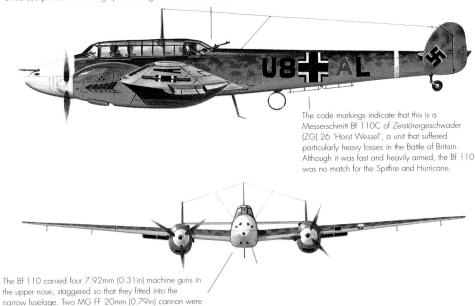

The code markings indicate that this is a Messerschmitt Bf 110C of *Zerstörergeschwader* (ZG) 26 'Horst Wessel', a unit that suffered particularly heavy losses in the Battle of Britain. Although it was fast and heavily armed, the Bf 110 was no match for the Spitfire and Hurricane.

The Bf 110 carried four 7.92mm (0.31in) machine guns in the upper nose, staggered so that they fitted into the narrow fuselage. Two MG FF 20mm (0.79in) cannon were mounted in the lower fuselage beneath the pilot's seat.

GERMANY

This Bf 110G-4/R3 was pictured while undergoing RAF tests at Farnborough.

Designed in response to a 1934 specification for a long-range escort fighter and *Zerstörer* (destroyer) aircraft, the Messerschmitt Bf 110 was also produced in bomber and reconnaissance sub-variants, despite suffering very serious losses as a day fighter in the Battle of Britain. The Bf 110D-1

was originally intended as a long-range escort fighter. The D-2 could be used in either the fighter or bomber roles, and the D-3 was a D-1 with bomb racks attached. The Bf 110E-1 and E-2 were able to carry four 50kg (110lb) bombs under the wing in addition to the larger bombs slung under the fuselage, while the E-3 was a special long-range reconnaissance model. The Bf 110F-1 (bomber), F-2 (heavy fighter), F-3 (long-range reconnaissance aircraft) and F-4 (night fighter) had 969kW (1300hp) DB 601F engines, but the final major production aircraft, the Bf 110G, produced in larger numbers than any other variant, adopted the 1007kW (1350hp) DB 605 engine. The Bf 110G-4 was a night fighter, and it was in this role that the Bf 110 truly excelled.

Messerschmitt Bf 110G

Powerplant:	two 1100kW (1475hp) Daimler-Benz DB 605B-1 12-cylinder inverted-Vee type engines
Performance:	maximum speed 550km/h (342mph) at 7000m (22,960ft); service ceiling 8000m (26,245ft); range 1300km (808 miles)
Weights:	empty 5094kg (11,232lb); maximum take-off 9888kg (21,799lb)
Dimensions:	wing span 16.25m (53ft 3.66in); length 13.05m (42ft 9.66in); height 4.18m (13ft 8.5in)
Armament:	two 30mm (1.19in) cannon, two 20mm (0.79in) cannon and one machine gun or two upward-firing 20mm (0.79in) cannon

Messerschmitt Bf 110s in flight over a Norwegian fjord. The aircraft nearest the camera belongs to ZG 26.

GERMANY

65

MESSERSCHMITT ME 163 KOMET

*The remarkable and revolutionary Me 163
rocket-powered interceptor was yet another example
of German ingenuity, but it
came too late to alter the
course of the air war.*

The Me 163C was to have
been fitted with a novel
armament arrangement
developed by Dr Langweiler
(inventor of the *Panzerfaust*
one-man anti-tank weapon)
comprising five vertically
mounted tubes in each wing,
each tube containing a 50mm
(1.97in) shell. The equipment
was activated by a photo-
electric cell as the rocket fighter
passed under an enemy
bomber.

The fuel used was a highly volatile mixture of *T-Stoff* (80 per cent hydrogen peroxide and 20 per cent water) and *C-Stoff* (hydrazine hydrate, methyl alcohol, and water).

With its 120 rounds of ammunition used up and its speed beginning to drop, the *Komet* would then dive steeply away from the combat area and glide back to base, landing on a skid. This in itself was a hazardous procedure, as there was always a risk of explosion if any unburnt rocket fuel remained in the aircraft's tanks. Many Me 163s were lost in landing accidents.

Taking off on its jettisonable trolley, the *Komet* would climb initially at 3600m/min (11,800ft/min), rising to 10,200m/min (33,470ft/min) at 9760m (32,020ft). Time to the *Komet's* operational ceiling of 12,100m (39,690ft) was a mere 3.35 minutes. Maximum powered endurance was eight minutes.

GERMANY

based on the experimental DFS 194, the first two Me 163 prototypes were flown in the spring of 1941 as unpowered gliders, the Me 163V-1 being transferred to Peenemunde later in the year to be fitted with its 750kg (1653lb) thrust Walter HWK R.II rocket motor. The first rocket-powered flight was made in August

The Me 163 rocket fighter was revolutionary, but dangerous to fly.

1941, and during subsequent trials the Me 163 broke all existing world air speed records, reaching speeds of up to 1000km/h (620mph). In May 1944, after operational trials with *Erprobungkommando* EK 16, an operational *Komet* unit, JG400, began forming at Wittmundhaven and Venlo, and in June all three *Staffeln* of this unit moved to Brandis near Leipzig, together with EK16.

NINE KILLS

The task of the *Komets* at Brandis was to defend the Leuna oil refinery, which lay 90km (55 miles) to the south. About 300 *Komets* were built, but JG400 remained the only operational unit and the rocket fighter recorded only nine kills during its brief career. The Me 163C, the last version to be built for operational use, had a pressurized cockpit, an improved Walter 109-509C

Messerschmitt Me 163B-1a

Powerplant:	1700kg (3749lb) thrust Walter 109-509A-2 rocket motor
Performance:	maximum speed 955km/h (593mph); service ceiling 12,000m (39,370ft); range 35.5km (22 miles)
Weights:	empty 1900kg (4190lb); maximum take-off 4310kg (9502lb)
Dimensions:	wing span 9.33m (30ft 7.5in); length 5.85m (19ft 2.25in); height 2.76m (9ft)
Armament:	two 30mm (1.19in) cannon

motor, and featured a bubble canopy on a slightly lengthened fuselage. Only a few examples were produced, and these were not issued to units.

The red-painted Me 163B-1a first flew operationally on 14 May 1944.

GERMANY

MESSERSCHMITT ME 262

*Had its development programme not been delayed,
the Me 262 jet fighter might have wrested air
superiority from the
Allies in 1944. As it was,
it posed a serious threat.*

The Me 262 was
powered by two axial-
flow compressor type
Junkers Jumo 004B
turbojets. They were very
unreliable and short-
lived, with a life of only
25 hours, and this
greatly reduced the
availability of Me 262s
for front-line units.

Although the pilot's cockpit
was narrow, the clear-view
canopy provided excellent
visibility. He was protected by
an armoured backplate and a
thick armoured windscreen.

This Me 262A-1a carries the insignia of *Jagdgeschwader* (JG) 7, the Luftwaffe's first and only fully operational jet fighter *Geschwader*. Its pilots included some of the world's first jet fighter aces.

The Me 262 was initially equipped with a reflector gunsight, but this was later replaced by the very accurate Askania EZ42 gyroscopic sight.

The Me 262 packed a powerful punch, four 30mm (1.19in) MK 108 cannon in the nose. There were 100 rounds per gun for the upper pair and 80 rounds per gun for the lower ones. Towards the end of the war, JG 7's aircraft were also armed with R4M rockets.

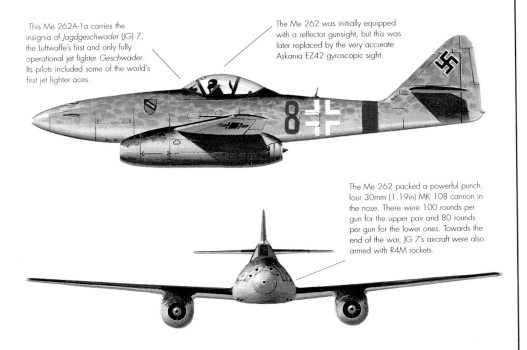

GERMANY

D esign work on the Me 262, the world's first operational jet fighter, began in September 1939, a month after the successful flight of the world's first jet aircraft, the Heinkel He 178. However, its development was protracted because of various factors, including problems with its turbojets and Hitler's later obsession with

The Me 262B-1a/U1 night fighter proved effective against the Mosquito.

using the aircraft as a bomber rather than a fighter. Because of the lack of jet engines the prototype Me 262V-1 flew on 18 April 1941 under the power of a Jumo 210G piston engine, and it was not until 18 July

1942 that the Me 262V-3 made a flight under turbojet power.

TOP-SCORING ACES

Two versions of the Me 262 were developed in parallel: the Me 262A-2a *Sturmvogel* (Stormbird) bomber variant and the Me 262A-1a fighter. There were also two reconnaissance versions, the Me 262A-1a/U3 and Me 262A-5a. The first *Jagdgeschwader* to arm with the Me 262 fighter was JG 7 'Hindenburg'. A second Me 262 jet fighter unit known as *Jagdverband* 44, was manned by 45 highly experienced pilots, many of them Germany's top-scoring aces. Several variants of the Me 262 were proposed,

Messerschmitt Me 262A-1a

Powerplant:	two 900kg (1985lb) thrust Junkers Jumo 109-004B4 turbojets
Performance:	maximum speed 870km/h (541mph) at 7000m (2,960ft); service ceiling 11,450m (37,565ft); range 1050km (652 miles)
Weights:	empty 4420kg (9742lb); maximum take-off 7130kg (15,720lb)
Dimensions:	wing span 12.51m (41ft 0.5in); length 10.60m (34ft 9.5in); height 3.83m (12ft 6.33in)
Armament:	four 30mm (1.19in) cannon; 24 air-to-air rockets on underwing racks

including the radar-equipped Me 262B-1a/U1 two-seat night fighter, which saw brief operational service from March 1945.

The Me 262's weakness was its turbines, which had a life of only 25 hours.

GERMANY

73

FIAT G.55 CENTAURO

The fighter aircraft developed by Fiat for the Italian Air Force in World War II were generally able to fight well, but they all had defects which made them vulnerable to Allied fighters.

The G.55 carried a heavy armament of three 20mm (0.79in) cannon and two 12.7mm (0.50in) machine guns, the latter mounted in the upper forward fuselage. One of the three cannon was centrally mounted to fire through the propeller boss.

This G.55 bears the markings of the Italian Socialist Republic (RSI), which continued to fight alongside the Germans after the Italian government concluded an armistice with the Allies. The green, white and red RSI flag is displayed on fuselage sides and tail, while the fascist markings are painted over and under the wings.

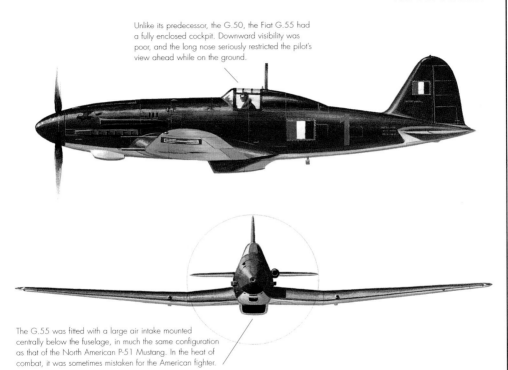

Unlike its predecessor, the G.50, the Fiat G.55 had a fully enclosed cockpit. Downward visibility was poor, and the long nose seriously restricted the pilot's view ahead while on the ground.

The G.55 was fitted with a large air intake mounted centrally below the fuselage, in much the same configuration as that of the North American P-51 Mustang. In the heat of combat, it was sometimes mistaken for the American fighter.

ITALY

This G.55 *Centauro* is pictured in German markings.

First tested in combat during the Spanish Civil War, the radial-engined Fiat G.50 subsequently saw service in North Africa, the Balkans and southern Russia. The basic soundness of its design persuaded Fiat to develop a successor with a higher performance and equipped with an inline engine. The aircraft that emerged

was the G.55 *Centauro*. Fitted with a DB.605A engine and featuring an enclosed cockpit, the G.55 was undoubtedly the best fighter produced in Italy during World War II, but it did not enter production until

1943, with the result that only a few had been delivered before the Armistice.

GOOD ACCOUNT

Production continued after this, however, and most of the 130 or so aircraft that were completed served with the pro-German Italian Socialist Republic forces, with whom they gave a good account of themselves against Allied fighters like the Spitfire and Mustang. The post-war Fiat G.59 trainer development of the G.55 was produced in single- and two-seat versions as the G.59A and G.59B. The G.59A was developed in response to an order for a combat version from Syria.

Fiat G.55 Centauro

Powerplant:	1100kW (1475hp) Daimler Benz DB 605A 12-cylinder V-type
Performance:	maximum speed 620km/h (385mph) at 7400m (24,300ft); service ceiling: 12,700m (41,700ft); range: 1650km (1025 miles)
Weights:	empty 2630kg (5799lb); maximum take-off 3718kg (8197lb)
Dimensions:	wing span 11.85m (38ft 10.5in); length 9.37m (30ft 9in); height 3.77m (12ft 4in)
Armament:	two 12.7mm (0.50in) machine guns and three 20mm (0.79in) cannon

The last variants were the single-seat G.59-4A and the G.59-4B two-seater; these appeared in 1951 and were fitted with a bubble canopy.

The Fiat G.59 was used post-war as a fighter trainer.

ITALY

SAVOIA-MARCHETTI SM.79 SPARVIERO

Of all the Italian bombers that served during World War II, the SM.79 Sparviero (Sparrowhawk) was probably the best known and most effective, especially in the role of torpedo-bomber.

The SM.79 carries the insignia of fascist Italy, the 'fasces' – a bundle of rods around an axe carried before a magistrate in ancient Rome as a symbol of authority. The symbol was adopted as the emblem of the Italian Fascist Party in the 1920s.

Defence of the upper rear of the aircraft was the responsibility of the flight engineer or radio operator, who used a 12.7mm (0.50in) gun on a flexible mount. The gun could be retracted and a panel put in place to cover the hole in the fuselage.

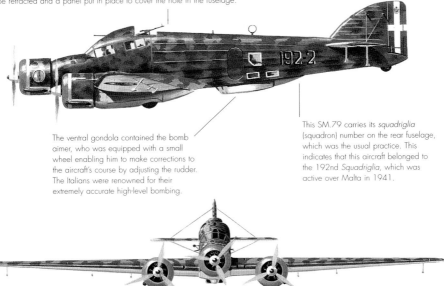

The ventral gondola contained the bomb aimer, who was equipped with a small wheel enabling him to make corrections to the aircraft's course by adjusting the rudder. The Italians were renowned for their extremely accurate high-level bombing.

This SM.79 carries its *squadriglia* (squadron) number on the rear fuselage, which was the usual practice. This indicates that this aircraft belonged to the 192nd *Squadriglia*, which was active over Malta in 1941.

ITALY

79

Ground crews wave off an SM.79 as it departs on a mission over North Africa.

Production of the SM.79 *Sparviero*, which was the military counterpart of an eight-seat civil airliner, began in October 1936 and was to have an uninterrupted run until June 1943, by which time 1217 aircraft had been built. The SM.79-II was equipped with 746kW (1000hp) Piaggio P.XI radial engines for the torpedo-bomber squadrons of the Regia Aeronautica, and it was in this role that the aircraft was to excel during World War II.

When Italy entered that conflict in June 1940, SM.79s of both variants accounted for well over half the Italian Air Force's total bomber strength. SM.79s saw continual action in the air campaign against Malta and in North Africa, becoming renowned for their high-level precision bombing, while the torpedo-bomber version was active against British shipping in the Aegean during the German invasion of Crete and against naval forces and convoys in the central Mediterranean.

The SM.79B, first flown in 1936, was a twin-engined export model, the middle engine being replaced by an extensively glazed nose, while the SM.84 was a version with twin fins.

Savoia-Marchetti SM.79-I *Sparviero*

Powerplant:	three 746kW (1000hp) Piaggio P.XI RC 40 radial engines
Performance:	maximum speed 435km/h (270mph) at 3650m (11,975ft); service ceiling 6500m (21,325ft); range: 1900km (1181 miles)
Weights:	empty 6800kg (14,991lb); maximum take-off 11,300kg (24,912lb)
Dimensions:	wing span 21.20m (69ft 6.5in); length 15.62m (51ft 3in); height 4.40m (14ft 5.25in)
Armament:	three 12.7mm (0.5in) machine guns and one 7.7mm (0.303in) machine gun; two 450mm (17.7in) torpedoes or 1250kg (2756lb) of bombs

The SM.79 performed very efficiently in the important torpedo-bomber role.

ITALY

81

AICHI D3A

Pictured here is an Aichi D3A1 of the Soryu Air Group, 1941. The Soryu formed part of the 1st Air Fleet and was one of the carriers in the task force that attacked Pearl Harbor.

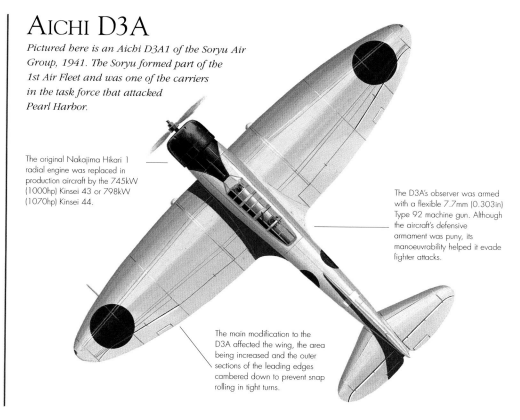

The original Nakajima Hikari 1 radial engine was replaced in production aircraft by the 745kW (1000hp) Kinsei 43 or 798kW (1070hp) Kinsei 44.

The D3A's observer was armed with a flexible 7.7mm (0.303in) Type 92 machine gun. Although the aircraft's defensive armament was puny, its manoeuvrability helped it evade fighter attacks.

The main modification to the D3A affected the wing, the area being increased and the outer sections of the leading edges cambered down to prevent snap rolling in tight turns.

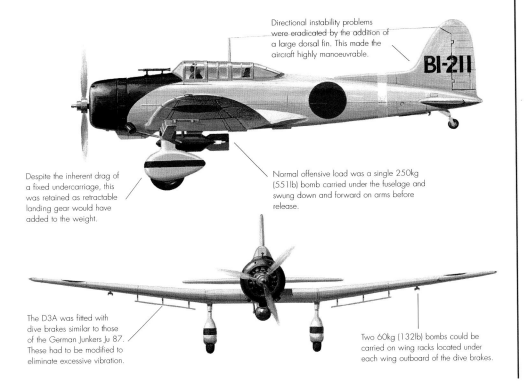

Directional instability problems were eradicated by the addition of a large dorsal fin. This made the aircraft highly manoeuvrable.

BI-211

Despite the inherent drag of a fixed undercarriage, this was retained as retractable landing gear would have added to the weight.

Normal offensive load was a single 250kg (551lb) bomb carried under the fuselage and swung down and forward on arms before release.

The D3A was fitted with dive brakes similar to those of the German Junkers Ju 87. These had to be modified to eliminate excessive vibration.

Two 60kg (132lb) bombs could be carried on wing racks located under each wing outboard of the dive brakes.

JAPAN

83

JAPAN

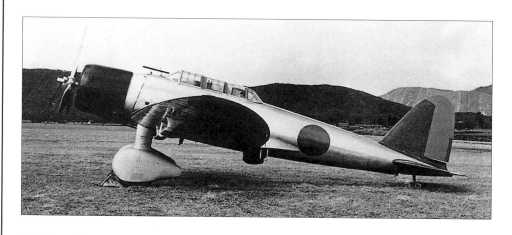

The second prototype Aichi 11-Shi, which developed into the D3A Type 99.

First flown in January 1938, the Aichi D3A dive-bomber, later given the Allied code-name Val, owed a great deal to German design philosophy. Its elliptical wing, in particular, reflected that of the Heinkel He 70 high-speed communications aircraft. After substantial modification to the prototypes, the design was ordered into production in December 1939 as the Navy Type 99 Carrer Bomber Model 11 (Aichi D3A1). The D3A1 saw limited action from land bases in China during the Sino–Japanese war.

STRENGTH IN NUMBERS

The D3A1 was the world's first all-metal low-wing monoplane dive-bomber, and was the most numerous of the aircraft used in the attack on Pearl Harbor on 7 December 1941, 126 taking part. In 1942 an improved version, the D3A2, made its appearance – fitted with a more powerful 969kW (1300hp) Kinsei engine and extra fuel tanks. By 1943, the design was obsolete and many were adapted to the training role as D3A2-K trainers. Production totalled 478 D3A1s and 816 D3A2s, many survivors

Aichi D3A1

Powerplant:	802kW (1075hp) Mitsubishi Kinsei 44 14-cylinder radial
Performance:	maximum speed 389km/h (242mph) at 3000m (9845ft); service ceiling: 9,500m (31,170ft); range 1131km (702 miles)
Weights:	empty 2570kg (5666lb); maximum take-off 3800kg (8378lb)
Dimensions:	Wing span 14.37m (47ft 2in) length 10.20m (33ft 5.5in); height 3.80m (12ft 5.5in)
Armament:	three 7.7mm (0.303in) machine guns plus external bomb load of 370kg (816lb)

being expended in *kamikaze* attacks at Leyte and Okinawa.

An Aichi D3A pulling away from a dive-bombing attack on Pearl Harbor.

JAPAN

KAWASAKI KI.45 TORYU

The Kawasaki Ki.45 Toryu, after a protracted development programme, became one of the most effective Japanese combat aircraft of World War II, but its full potential was never realized.

The night fighter version of the *Toryu* was equipped with a pair of 20mm (0.79in) cannon, obliquely mounted in the upper fuselage between the two cockpits, enabling the pilot to attack an enemy bomber from below.

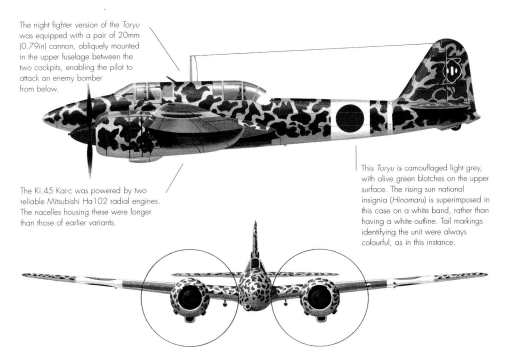

The Ki.45 Kai-c was powered by two reliable Mitsubishi Ha102 radial engines. The nacelles housing these were longer than those of earlier variants.

This *Toryu* is camouflaged light grey, with olive green blotches on the upper surface. The rising sun national insignia (*Hinomaru*) is superimposed in this case on a white band, rather than having a white outline. Tail markings identifying the unit were always colourful, as in this instance.

arly in 1937, the Imperial Japanese Army ordered Kawasaki to initiate the design and development of a twin-engined heavy fighter, in the same category as Germany's Messerschmitt 110, that would be suitable for long-range operations over the Pacific. The result was the Kawasaki Ki.45 *Toryu* (Dragon Slayer), the prototype

This is probably the best surviving photograph of a Kawasaki Ki.45.

for which flew in January 1939. Five more prototypes were built, and trials revealed problems with both the landing gear and engines. Flight testing was resumed in July 1940, but the development programme continued slowly and the aircraft did not enter service until the autumn of 1942 as the Ki.45 Kai-a fighter and the Ki.45 Kai-b ground-attack and anti-shipping strike aircraft, the 'Kai' suffix denoting 'improved'. The Ki.45 Kai-c was a night fighter version, while the Kai-d was an improved ground-attack/anti-shipping variant. The *Toryu* was one of the most effective Japanese home defence night fighters, but its efficiency was hampered by the lack of a modern early warning and interception radar system. Many aircraft of this type were expended in *kamikaze* attacks during the final months of the war. Total production of the *Toryu* was 1675 aircraft, of which 477 were night fighters. The *Toryu* received the Allied codename Nick.

Kawasaki Ki.45 Kai-c

Powerplant:	two 805kW (1080hp) Mitsubishi Ha-102 14-cylinder radials
Performance:	maximum speed 540km/h (336mph) at 5000m (16,405ft); service ceiling 10,000m (32,810ft); range 2000km (1243 miles)
Weights:	empty 4000kg (8820lb); maximum take-off 5500kg (12,125lb) loaded
Dimensions:	wing span 15.02m (49ft 3in); length 11.00m (36ft 1in); height 3.70m (12ft 1.33in)
Armament:	one 37mm (1.46in) cannon, two 20mm (0.79in) cannon and one 7.92mm (0.31in) machine gun

The Ki.45 was Japan's only night fighter, and proved very effective.

JAPAN

89

KAWASAKI KI.61 HIEN

*Designed to replace the Nakajima Ki.43
Hayabusa (Oscar) in Japanese army
service, The Kawasaki Ki.61 began
to reach front-line air units in
August 1942.*

The Ki.61 Daimler-Benz
DB.601A was chosen
because reports from the air
fighting in Europe seemed to
indicate that the liquid-cooled
engine was superior to the air-
cooled variety. Blueprints were
brought back from Germany
by a Japanese technical team
in April 1940, and several
assembled engines were
imported to serve as patterns
for licence production.

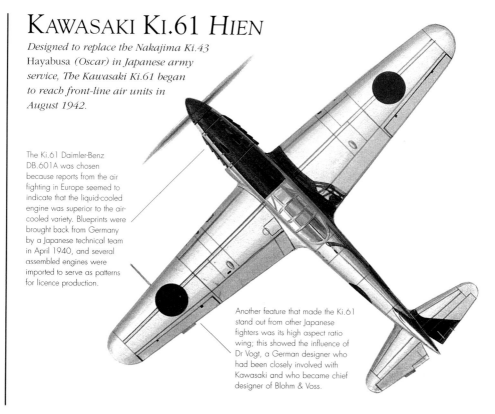

Another feature that made the Ki.61
stand out from other Japanese
fighters was its high aspect ratio
wing; this showed the influence of
Dr Vogt, a German designer who
had been closely involved with
Kawasaki and who became chief
designer of Blohm & Voss.

The Hien was armed with four 12.7mm (0.50in) machine guns, two of which were mounted in the upper forward fuselage. Some Ki.61-I fighters were armed with German 20mm (0.79in) Mauser MG 151/20 cannon, 400 of which were imported.

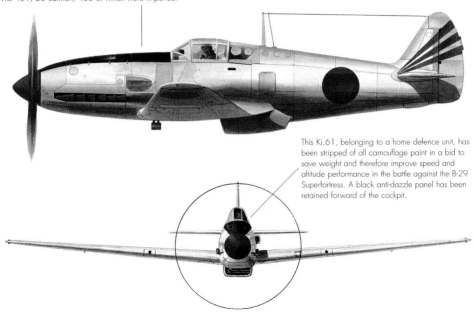

This Ki.61, belonging to a home defence unit, has been stripped of all camouflage paint in a bid to save weight and therefore improve speed and altitude performance in the battle against the B-29 Superfortress. A black anti-dazzle panel has been retained forward of the cockpit.

JAPAN

91

Ki.61 *Hien* fighters preparing to take off. The *Hien* employed a licence-built Daimler-Benz DB.601A engine.

Given the Japanese name *Hien* (Swallow) and known to the Allies as Tony, the Ki.61 was the only operational Japanese fighter to feature an inverted-V engine (a licence-built DB 601), and until Allied pilots became familiar with it its appearance gave rise to erroneous reports that the Japanese were using Messerschmitt Bf 109s. (In fact, the Bf 109 had been considered for production as the Japanese Army's primary interceptor in 1940, but the Nakajima Ki.44 Shoki was chosen in preference.) The prototype *Hien* flew in December 1941 and the aircraft went into full production some six months later. It was unique among Japanese fighter aircraft of World War II in that it marked the first attempt by the Japanese Army Air Force to incorporate armour protection and self-sealing fuel tanks into the design from the outset, measures shown to be vital by reports of the air fighting in Europe. By the end of the Pacific war 3028 Ki.61s had been built, serving in all areas. The principal versions were the Ki.61-I (1380 aircraft built in two sub-variants, differentiated by their armament); the Ki.61 Kai, with a lengthened fuselage and different armament fits (1274 built); and the Ki.61-II, optimized

Kawasaki Ki.61

Powerplant:	876kW (1175hp) Kawasaki Ha.40 12-cylinder inverted-V
Performance:	maximum speed 592km/h (368mph) at 5000m (16,405ft); service ceiling 11,500m (37,730ft); range 1100km (684 miles)
Weights:	empty 2210kg (4873lb); maximum take-off 3250kg (7165lb)
Dimensions:	wing span 12.00m (39ft 4.5in); length 8.75m (28ft 8.5in); height 3.70m (12ft 1.33in)
Armament:	four 12.7mm (0.50in) machine guns

for high altitude operation with a Kawasaki Ha.140 engine (374 built).

Many Japanese home defence fighters had colourful markings, as shown here.

JAPAN

MITSUBISHI A6M2 REISEN (ZERO FIGHTER)

The Mitsubishi Zero, also known as Zeke to the Allies, ruled the Pacific skies until the advent of Allied fighters that were a match for it.

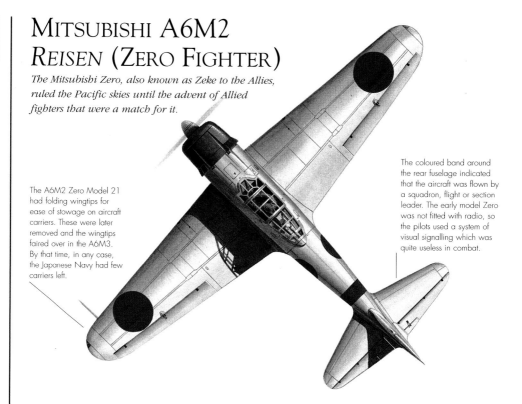

The A6M2 Zero Model 21 had folding wingtips for ease of stowage on aircraft carriers. These were later removed and the wingtips faired over in the A6M3. By that time, in any case, the Japanese Navy had few carriers left.

The coloured band around the rear fuselage indicated that the aircraft was flown by a squadron, flight or section leader. The early model Zero was not fitted with radio, so the pilots used a system of visual signalling which was quite useless in combat.

AF-152

The code letters and numerals on the Zero's tail identify the aircraft's unit. This one belongs to the fighter component of the air group aboard the aircraft carrier *Akagi*, which was involved in the attack on Pearl Harbor and was sunk at Midway six months later.

The pilot of the Zero did not have the benefit of armour protection, nor did the aircraft have self-sealing fuel tanks. This was a weight-saving measure, but Japanese psychology also came into play; it was unthinkable that a Japanese pilot might find himself in a position where he might be shot down.

As the Zero was originally intended as a long-range bomber escort, an under-fuselage fuel tank was standard equipment. The Japanese used long-range auxiliary tanks long before their western counterparts.

JAPAN

One of the finest fighter aircraft of all time, the Mitsubishi A6M *Reisen* (Zero) first flew on 1 April 1939. The Zero was accepted for service with the Japanese Naval Air Force in July 1940, entering full production in November that year as the A6M2 Model 11. Sixty-four Model 11s were completed, powered by the more

The A6M2 *Reisen* pioneered long-range flying procedures and techniques.

powerful Sakae 12 engine, and were followed by the Model 21 with folding wingtips. This was the major production version at the time of the attack on Pearl Harbor in December 1941. The A6M2 soon showed itself to be clearly superior to any fighter the Allies could put into the air in the early stages of the Pacific war.

KAMIKAZE ATTACKS

Its main drawback was that it had no armour plating and no self-sealing fuel tanks, which was to cost it heavily in combat. Other variants of the Zero included the A6M3, which originally had squared-off wingtips; the A6M5; the A6M7 (designed for *kamikaze* attacks), the A6M8, with a 1119kW (1500hp) Mitsubishi Kinsei 62 engine and four wing guns; a twin-float seaplane, the A6M2-N; and the A6M2-K2 two-

Mitsubishi A6M2 *Reisen*

Powerplant:	708kW (950hp) Nakajima NK1C Sakae 12 14-cylinder radial
Performance:	maximum speed 534km/h (332mph) at 4550m (14,930ft); service ceiling 10,000m (32,810ft); range 3104km (1929 miles)
Weights:	empty 1680kg (3704lb); maximum loaded 2796kg (6164lb)
Dimensions:	wing span 12.00m (39ft 4.5in); length 9.06m (29ft 8.33in); height 3.05m (10ft)
Armament:	two 20mm (0.79in) cannon and two 7.7mm (0.303in) machine guns plus external bomb load of 120kg (265lb)

seat trainer. In all, 10,937 Zeros of all versions were built.

A rare example of a captured A6M5 Zero, undergoing tests in the US.

JAPAN

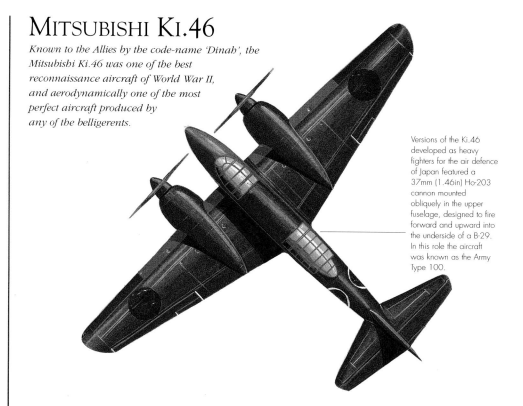

MITSUBISHI KI.46

*Known to the Allies by the code-name 'Dinah', the
Mitsubishi Ki.46 was one of the best
reconnaissance aircraft of World War II,
and aerodynamically one of the most
perfect aircraft produced by
any of the belligerents.*

Versions of the Ki.46
developed as heavy
fighters for the air defence
of Japan featured a
37mm (1.46in) Ho-203
cannon mounted
obliquely in the upper
fuselage, designed to fire
forward and upward into
the underside of a B-29.
In this role the aircraft
was known as the Army
Type 100.

The Ki.46's pilot and gunner were seated in two cockpits separated by a large fuel tank. To meet performance requirements, the aircraft's designers adopted a fuselage of small diameter.

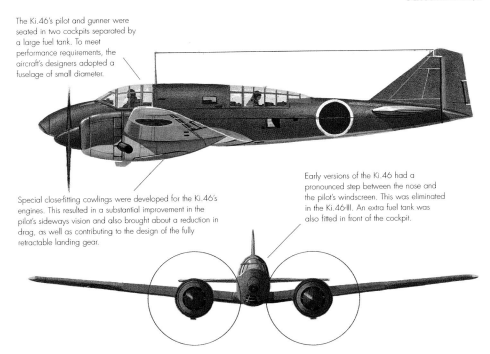

Special close-fitting cowlings were developed for the Ki.46's engines. This resulted in a substantial improvement in the pilot's sideways vision and also brought about a reduction in drag, as well as contributing to the design of the fully retractable landing gear.

Early versions of the Ki.46 had a pronounced step between the nose and the pilot's windscreen. This was eliminated in the Ki.46-III. An extra fuel tank was also fitted in front of the cockpit.

JAPAN

JAPAN

The design of the Mitsubishi Ki.46 owed much to studies carried out by the Institute of Aeronautical Research at the University of Tokyo in 1938–39. The prototype flew for the first time in November 1939 and was followed by a small production batch of 34 Ki.46-I aircraft with 671kW (900hp) Mitsubishi Ha.26-I radial engines.

A Mitsubishi Ki.46-IV, powered by two supercharged Ha-112-II Ru engines, giving better performance at altitude.

Production then switched to the first fully operational model, the Ki.46-II, 1093 examples of which were built. Such was the success of this aircraft that at one point a technical mission from Germany seriously considered applying for a production licence.

REDESIGNED NOSE

A further version, the Ki.46-IIIa, appeared in 1943; this featured a redesigned all-glazed nose section, 654 being built. The Ki.46-III-Kai was an interceptor version with a 'solid' nose, mounting a 37mm (1.47in) cannon and either two 20mm (0.79in) cannon or two 12.7mm (0.50in) machine guns, while the similarly armed Ki.46-IIIb was a ground-attack aircraft. Production of all versions totalled 1783 aircraft, including three Ki.46-IVa machines with turbocharged engines.

Mitsubishi Ki.46-III

Powerplant:	two 787kW (1055hp) Mitsubishi Ha.102 14-cylinder radials
Performance:	maximum speed 604km/h (375mph) at 8000m (26,245ft); service ceiling 10,720m (35,170ft); range 2474km (1537 miles)
Weights:	empty 3263kg (7194lb); maximum take-off 5800kg (12,789lb)
Dimensions:	wing span 14.70m (48ft 2.33in); length 11.00m (36ft 1in); height 3.88m (12ft 8.75in)
Armament:	one 7.7mm (0.303in) machine gun

The Ki.46-III-Kai was thrown into battle against the B-29 bombers that were attacking Japan on an almost daily basis in 1945.

A Mitsubishi Ki.46-III-Kai, also called the Army Type 100 Air Defence Fighter.

JAPAN

MITSUBISHI KI.67 *HIRYU*

Although classed as a heavy bomber, the Mitsubishi Ki.67 was roughly in the same class as the Martin B-26 Marauder.
An excellent design, it appeared too late to have a decisive effect on the Pacific air war.

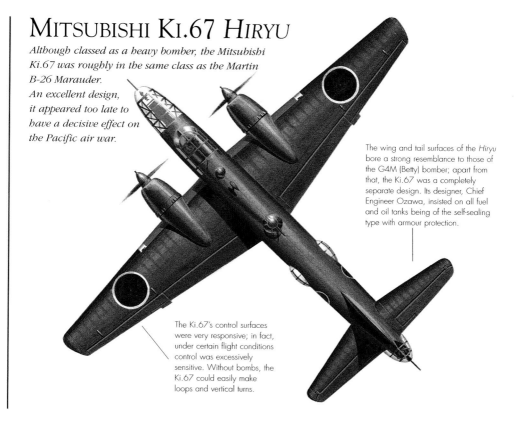

The wing and tail surfaces of the *Hiryu* bore a strong resemblance to those of the G4M (Betty) bomber; apart from that, the Ki.67 was a completely separate design. Its designer, Chief Engineer Ozawa, insisted on all fuel and oil tanks being of the self-sealing type with armour protection.

The Ki.67's control surfaces were very responsive; in fact, under certain flight conditions control was excessively sensitive. Without bombs, the Ki.67 could easily make loops and vertical turns.

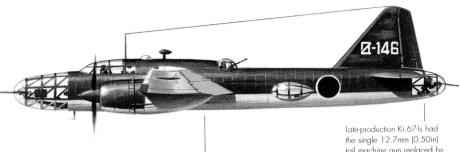

The *Hiryu* had a respectable bomb load and a capacious weapons bay. Ki.67s operated in China, and in 1945, using Iwo Jima as a refuelling point, they made repeated attacks on B-29 bases in the Marianas.

Late-production Ki.67-Is had the single 12.7mm (0.50in) tail machine gun replaced by a twin mounting, starting with the 451st Mitsubishi-built machine.

JAPAN

The Ki.67 *Hiryu* (Flying Dragon) was unquestionably the best bomber to see service with the Imperial Japanese Army, combining excellent performance with good defensive firepower. Its main drawback was that by the time it made its appearance, the only crews available to fly it were generally

Although originally classed as a heavy bomber, the Ki.67 had relatively small dimensions compared to Allied types.

young and inexperienced, the best men having long since been sacrificed. The prototype flew in December 1942 but development was protracted and deliveries of fully operational Ki.67-I aircraft did not begin until the summer of 1944. The initial Ki.67-Ia was quickly supplanted by the Ki.67-Ib, which remained in production until the end of the war. Production totalled 698 aircraft, serving as bombers, torpedo-bombers, reconnaissance aircraft, interceptors, ground-attack aircraft and suicide bombers. The interceptor version was designated Ki.109 and was not a success, only 22 being completed. As a torpedo-bomber, the Ki.67 was particularly active during the air-sea battle off Formosa in October 1944 and during the American landings on Okinawa, being operated by both Japanese Army and Navy units. The *Hiryu* was known by the Allied code-name Peggy.

Mitsubishi Ki.67-I

Powerplant:	two 1417kW (1900hp) Mitsubishi Ha.104 18-cylinder radials
Performance:	maximum speed 537km/h (334mph) at 6000m (19,685ft); service ceiling 9470m (31,069ft); range 3800km (2361 miles)
Weights:	empty 8650kg (19,073lb); maximum take-off 13,765kg (30,347lb)
Dimensions:	wing span 22.50m (73ft 9.33in); length 18.70m (61ft 4.25in); height 7.70m (25ft 3in)
Armament:	one 20mm (0.79in) cannon and five 12.7mm (0.50in) machine guns; bomb or torpedo load of 1070kg (2359lb)

A Ki.67 of the Imperial Japanese Army Air Force.

JAPAN

NAKAJIMA B5N2

At the outbreak of the Pacific war, the Nakajima B5N
was the most effective and modern torpedo-bomber
in service anywhere in the world.

The B5N2 had a crew of three in
a fully enclosed cockpit, comprising
the pilot, an observer/navigator
who also acted as bomb aimer,
and the radio operator, who also
manned the trainable 7.7mm
(0.303in) machine gun that was
the aircraft's sole means of defence.

The B5N was tested in two
versions, one with Fowler-type
flaps, hydraulic flaps and
hydraulic wing folding, and
the other with plain flaps and
manual wing folding. It was
the latter version that was
ordered into production.

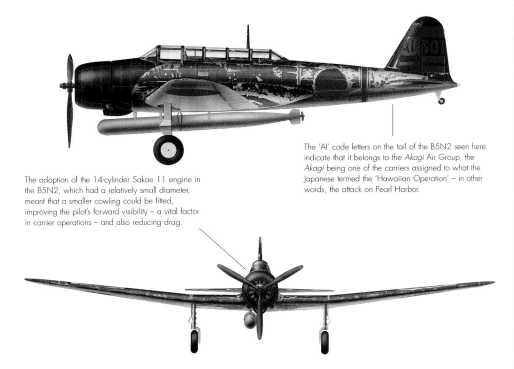

The adoption of the 14-cylinder Sakae 11 engine in the B5N2, which had a relatively small diameter, meant that a smaller cowling could be fitted, improving the pilot's forward visibility – a vital factor in carrier operations – and also reducing drag.

The 'AI' code letters on the tail of the B5N2 seen here indicate that it belongs to the *Akagi* Air Group, the *Akagi* being one of the carriers assigned to what the Japanese termed the 'Hawaiian Operation' – in other words, the attack on Pearl Harbor.

JAPAN

Designed in 1936, the prototype B5N carrier attack bomber made its maiden flight in January 1937 and became operational as the B5N1 light bomber during the Sino-Japanese war. After its usefulness in that conflict was assessed, no major modifications were found necessary, but the need to improve

The Nakajima B5N2 performed well in the Japanese attack on Pearl Harbor.

the aircraft's performance was apparent. This led to a more powerful version, the B5N2. Most of the B5N1s were allocated to the training role as they were progressively replaced by the B5N2 in 1939–40.

FATAL BLOWS

The B5N2 was one of the principal aircraft involved in the attack on Pearl Harbor on 7 December 1941, 144 machines taking part in the strike, and in the year that followed B5N2s delivered fatal blows to the US aircraft carriers *Lexington*, *Yorktown* and *Hornet*, as well as supporting Japanese amphibious assaults. The B5N2 remained in production until 1943, by which time 1149 examples of both variants had been built. Many B5Ns were later assigned to anti-submarine patrol work, after staggering losses sustained during the battle for the Philippines. Some were equipped with

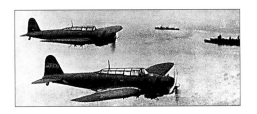

Nakajima B5N2

Powerplant:	746kW (1000hp) Nakajima NK1B Sakae 11 14-cylinder radial
Performance:	maximum speed 378km/h (235mph) at 3600m (11,811ft); service ceiling 8260m (27,100ft); range 2000km (1243 miles)
Weights:	empty 2279kg (5025lb); maximum take-off 4108kg (9056lb)
Dimensions:	wing span 15.51m (50ft 11in); length 10.30m (33ft 9.5in); height 3.70m (12ft 1.33in)
Armament:	one 7.7mm (0.303in) machine gun; one 800kg (1764lb) torpedo, or up to 800kg (1764lb) of bombs

rudimentary ASV (air to surface vessel) radar. The B5N2 was known to the Allies as Kate.

This photograph shows two early-model B5N1s over units of the Japanese fleet.

JAPAN

NAKAJIMA KI.43 HAYABUSA

*Like its naval counterpart, the Mitsubishi Zero, the
Nakajima Ki.43* Hayabusa *(Allied code-name Oscar)
was in action from the first day of Japan's war
until the last, by which time it was
woefully outclassed by the latest
Allied fighters.*

The initial production
variant, designated Army
Type 1 Fighter Model 1A,
was fitted with a fixed-pitch
two-blade wooden
propeller, but this was soon
replaced by a two-pitch
two-blade metal unit.

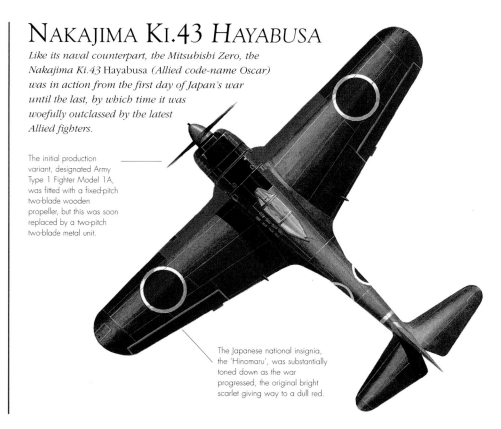

The Japanese national insignia,
the 'Hinomaru', was substantially
toned down as the war
progressed, the original bright
scarlet giving way to a dull red.

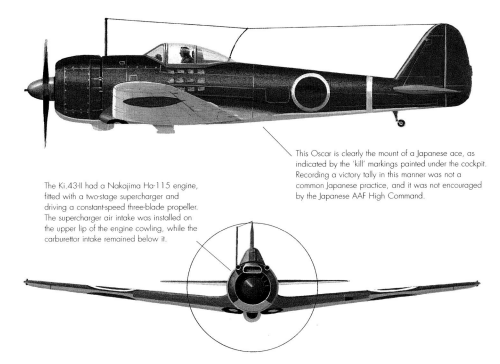

This Oscar is clearly the mount of a Japanese ace, as indicated by the 'kill' markings painted under the cockpit. Recording a victory tally in this manner was not a common Japanese practice, and it was not encouraged by the Japanese AAF High Command.

The Ki.43-II had a Nakajima Ha-115 engine, fitted with a two-stage supercharger and driving a constant-speed three-blade propeller. The supercharger air intake was installed on the upper lip of the engine cowling, while the carburettor intake remained below it.

The prototype Ki.43 flew in early January 1939 and 716 early production models were produced. These were the Ki.43-I, K.43-Ia, Ki.43-Ib and Ki.43-Ic, the last two having a better armament. They were followed in 1942 by a much improved model, the Ki.43-II; this appeared in three sub-variants, the Ki.43-IIa

Ki.43 *Hayabusa* fighters at a fighter training school in Japan.

and -IIb, and the Ki.43-Kai, which adopted all the refinements incorporated in the earlier models. The final model was the Ki.43-III, the only variant to include cannon in its armament. Production of all versions totalled 5878 aircraft, including 3200 by Nakajima and 2629 by Tachikawa. The *Hayabusa* was the Allies' principal opponent in Burma and was encountered in large numbers in the battle for Leyte, in the Philippines, and in the defence of the Kurile Islands north of Japan.

An excellent and versatile fighter, the *Hayabusa*'s main drawback was its lack of adequate armament and any form of armour protection, which made it extremely vulnerable. The type was operated by the Royal Thai Air Force during the war, and was flown post-war by pilots of the Indonesian People's Security Force against the Dutch, who were attempting to re-establish colonial

Nakajima Ki.43-IIb *Hayabusa*

Powerplant:	858kW (1150hp) Nakajima Ha.115 14-cylinder radial
Performance:	maximum speed 530km/h (329mph) at 5000m (16,405ft); service ceiling 11,200m (36,750ft); range 3200km (1990 miles)
Weights:	empty 1910kg (4211lb); maximum take-off 2925kg (6450lb)
Dimensions:	wing span 10.84m (35ft 6.33in); length 8.92m (29ft 3.25in); height 3.27m (10ft 8.33in)
Armament:	two 12.7mm (0.50in) machine guns plus external bomb load of 500kg (1102lb)

rule in what was then the Netherlands East Indies.

A Ki.43-I-Hei of the 64th Sentai, operating in Burma in 1943–44.

JAPAN

113

YOKOSUKA MXY7 OHKA

The notion of a pilot deliberately sacrificing his life as an act of war was foreign to western minds in World War II, but the Japanese brought the concept to grim reality in their Special Attack Corps, whose ultimate development was the Ohka *suicide bomb.*

The initial version of the *Ohka* was fitted with a 1200kg (2646lb) warhead and was designed to be transported to within a few miles of its target in the bomb bay of a specially modified Navy Type 1 Attack Bomber Model 24J (G4M2e).

The wing span of the *Ohka* Model 22, an improved version, was less than that of the Model 11, and its warhead limited to 600kg (1323lb). This version was to have been powered by a turbojet engine.

After release from its parent aircraft, the *Ohka* accelerated towards its target under the power of three solid-propellant rockets mounted in the tail, which could be fired either singly or together.

The tiny aircraft was built of wood and non-critical metal alloys, and great care was taken in planning to enable it to be mass-produced by unskilled labour.

As the aircraft was to be flown on its one-way mission by pilots with only limited flying experience, instruments were kept to a minimum and good manoeuvrability was required to achieve accuracy. Once the cockpit hood was bolted into place, there was no escape for the pilot.

JAPAN

115

A stockpiled *Ohka* suicide bomb ready to be used against an invasion force.

One of the more sinister weapons to emerge from World War II, the unpowered prototype MXY7 *Ohka* (Cherry Blossom) suicide aircraft flew in October 1944 and was followed by 45 of the *Ohka* K-1 training model, which was also unpowered. The rocket-powered production model was the *Ohka* Model 11, of which 755 were built between September 1944 and March 1945. The *Ohka* went into action for the first time on 21 March 1945, but the 16 Mitsubishi G4M2e parent aircraft (which carried the *Ohka*s shackled under the open bomb bay) were intercepted and forced to release their bombs short of the target. The first success came on 1 April, when *Ohka*s damaged the battleship *West Virginia* and three transport vessels. The first ship to be destroyed by an *Ohka* was the destroyer *Mannert L. Abele*, lost off Okinawa on 12 April. Several further versions of the *Ohka* were proposed, including the turbojet-powered Model 33, but none materialized in operational form before the end of the war. In objective military terms the concept of the *Ohka* was sound enough, but the lack of suitable carrier aircraft meant the weapon consistently failed to break through the

Yokosuka MXY7 *Ohka* Model 11

Powerplant:	three solid-fuel Type 4 Mk 1 Model 20 rockets with total thrust of 800kg (1764lb)
Performance:	maximum speed 927km/h (576mph) in terminal dive; range: 37km (23 miles)
Weights:	empty 440kg (970lb); loaded 2140kg (4718lb)
Dimensions:	wing span 5.12m (16ft 9.5in); length 6.07m (19ft 10.33in); height 1.16m (3ft 9.5in)
Armament:	one 1200kg (2646lb) warhead

Allied fighter screen. A long-range version and one intended to be catapulted from a surfaced submarine were under development when the war ended.

The *Ohka* was not a success due to the lack of a specialist carrier aircraft.

JAPAN

PZL P.11c

The gull-winged monoplane fighters produced by the Polish Panstowe Zaklady Lotnicze *(National Aviation Establishments) during the inter-war years were among the best in service with any air force, but they were outmoded by the time Germany invaded Poland in 1939.*

The P.11c was powered by the extremely reliable Bristol Mercury radial engine, which was also the powerplant chosen for aircraft like Britain's Gloster Gladiator biplane fighter. The Mercury was a major British aero-engine success story, with sales all over the world in the 1930s.

118

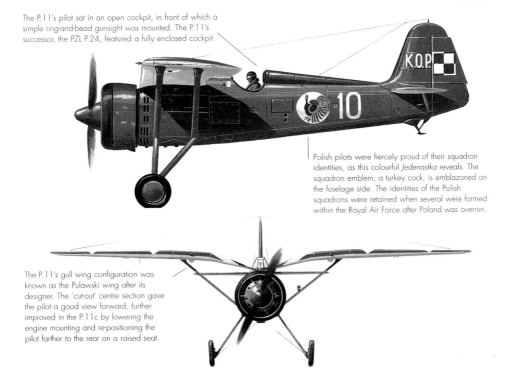

The P.11's pilot sat in an open cockpit, in front of which a simple ring-and-bead gunsight was mounted. The P.11's successor, the PZL P.24, featured a fully enclosed cockpit.

Polish pilots were fiercely proud of their squadron identities, as this colourful *Jedenastka* reveals. The squadron emblem, a turkey cock, is emblazoned on the fuselage side. The identities of the Polish squadrons were retained when several were formed within the Royal Air Force after Poland was overrun.

The P.11's gull wing configuration was known as the Pulawski wing after its designer. The 'cut-out' centre section gave the pilot a good view forward, further improved in the P.11c by lowering the engine mounting and re-positioning the pilot farther to the rear on a raised seat.

The gull-winged PZL P.11 was a more powerful derivative of the PZL P.7, which equipped all first-line fighter squadrons of the Polish Air Force's 1st, 2nd, 3rd and 4th Air Regiments at the end of 1933 and was one of the best fighter aircraft of its day. Its successor, the PZL P.11, was basically a more powerful derivative which

Although an excellent design, the P.11 was no match for the Luftwaffe.

first flew in September 1931, with deliveries beginning in 1934. Most P.11s were powered by Bristol Mercury engines built under licence by Skoda. The definitive version of the fighter was the P.11c, of which 175 were built. The P.11 was to have been replaced by a low-wing fighter monoplane, the P.50 *Jastrzeb* (Hawk), as part of a major expansion scheme, but cuts in the military budget resulted in the cancellation of an order for 300 P.50s, and more P.11s were purchased instead. They suffered heavy losses during the German invasion of Poland in September 1939.

The P.11b was an export model for Romania, which also built a small number of the type under licence as the P.11f. The P.24, which appeared in 1933, was basically similar but had a 574kW (770hp) Gnome-

PZL P.11c

Powerplant:	418kW (560hp) Bristol Mercury VS2 radial
Performance:	maximum speed 370km/h (230mph) at 4500m (14,764ft); service ceiling 9500m (31,170ft); range 810km (503 miles)
Weights:	empty 1147kg (2529lb); maximum take-off 1590kg (3505lb)
Dimensions:	wing span 10.72m (35ft 2in); length 7.55m (24ft 9.25in); height 2.85m (9ft 4.25in)
Armament:	two 7.7mm (0.303in) machine guns

Rhone 14K engine and featured an enclosed cockpit. The P.24 never served in the Polish Air Force, but was used by Turkey, Romania, Greece and Bulgaria.

The P.11 was powered by the very reliable Bristol Mercury engine.

ILYUSHIN IL-2 STURMOVIK

In its early combat career the Il-2 Sturmovik *was easy prey for Luftwaffe fighter pilots, but progressive refinements turned it into one of the world's most potent ground-attack aircraft.*

The circular metal tube projecting from the Sturmovik's spinner is not a cannon or machine gun, but a Hucks starter dog used for turning over and firing the engine, in much the same way as a vehicle starting handle.

For winter operations, Il-2s were camouflaged in a soluble white paintwork over their normal green-brown finish. The red star insignia was not carried on the upper surfaces of the wings, being highly visible to fighters patrolling at higher altitude.

Early Il-2 aircraft, like the one seen here, were single-seaters, which made them vulnerable to the Luftwaffe's fighters. A rear gun position had actually been built into the original design, but deleted in the course of development.

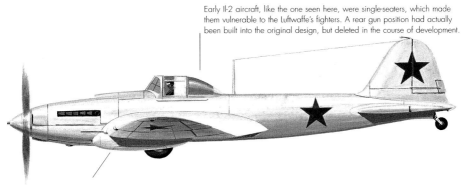

The large undercarriage fairings of the Il-2 left the undercarriage partially uncovered, which meant that a pilot could make a belly landing without causing too much damage to the aircraft. Passengers are known to have been carried in the fairings in extreme circumstances (the rescue of a downed pilot, for example), the undercarriage remaining in the down position.

SOVIET UNION

123

Destined to become one of the most famous ground-attack aircraft of all time, the Ilyushin Il-2 completed its State Acceptance Trials in March 1941 and was ordered into full production, 249 being produced before the German invasion of June 1941. It suffered serious losses in its early operational career, mainly because it

The Ilyushin Il-10, a post-war development of the Il-2.

lacked a rear gun position, and despite various improvements to the single-seater, it was not until August 1943 that a two-seater version made its appearance. This was the Il-2m3, which thereafter played a prominent, and often decisive, part in the campaigns on the Eastern Front.

The *Sturmovik* is probably best remembered for its part in the Battle of Kursk in the summer of 1943, when its concentrated attacks virtually destroyed the German 3rd Panzer Division and inflicted severe losses on 2nd Panzer. By the winter of 1943–44 vast numbers of Il-2m3s were in service, equipping units of the Soviet Naval Air Arm as well as the Soviet Air Force. The number of Il-2s built reached the staggering total of 36,183, more than any other aircraft in history.

Ilyushin Il-2m3

Powerplant:	1320kW (1770hp) Mikulin AM-38F liquid-cooled inline engine
Performance:	maximum speed 404km/h (251mph) at 760m (2500ft); service ceiling 6000m (19,685ft); range: 800km (497 miles)
Weights:	empty 4525kg (9976lb); maximum take-off 6360kg (14,023lb)
Dimensions:	wing span 14.60m (47ft 10.33in); length 11.60m (38ft 0.5in); height 3.40m (11ft 1.5in)
Armament:	(typical) two 37mm (1.46in) and two 7.62mm (0.30in) machine guns; one 12.7mm (0.50in) machine gun, plus 200 hollow-charge anti-tank bombs, or eight rocket projectiles

Ilyushin Il-2m3s pictured over the Eastern Front in late 1944.

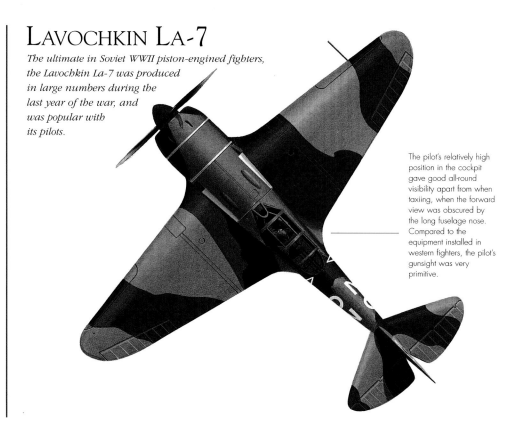

LAVOCHKIN LA-7

*The ultimate in Soviet WWII piston-engined fighters,
the Lavochkin La-7 was produced
in large numbers during the
last year of the war, and
was popular with
its pilots.*

The pilot's relatively high
position in the cockpit
gave good all-round
visibility apart from when
taxiing, when the forward
view was obscured by
the long fuselage nose.
Compared to the
equipment installed in
western fighters, the pilot's
gunsight was very
primitive.

The La-7 carried two guns in its upper fuselage decking, synchronized to fire through the propeller disc. The guns were 20mm (0.79in) ShVAK cannon and had 200 rounds of ammunition each.

Both the La-5FN and La-7 were powered by the Shvetsov M-82FN radial engine. It had two banks of seventeen cylinders each, with two-stage supercharging and direct fuel injection.

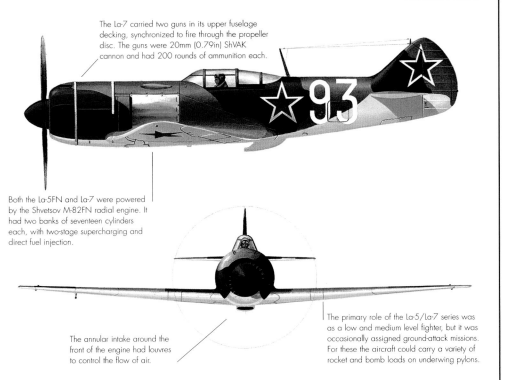

The annular intake around the front of the engine had louvres to control the flow of air.

The primary role of the La-5/La-7 series was as a low and medium level fighter, but it was occasionally assigned ground-attack missions. For these the aircraft could carry a variety of rocket and bomb loads on underwing pylons.

The Lavochkin La-7 was a variant of the earlier La-5, differing in only minor detail. The La-5 itself was developed from the earlier LaGG-3 in response to a desperate requirement for the Soviet Air Force, which had suffered appalling casualties at the hands of the Luftwaffe in the second half of 1941, for a

The Lavochkin La-5 played a pivotal role in the defence of the Soviet Union.

modern fighter that could hold its own against the Bf 109. Lavochkin retained the basic LaGG-3 airframe, and married it with a 992kW (1330hp) M-82F radial engine. Other modifications included a cut-down rear fuselage, providing much-improved pilot visibility, and a heavier armament. Early combats showed that the La-5 was a better all-round performer than the Bf 109G, although its rate of climb was inferior. To improve its performance, Lavochkin fitted the fighter with a 1126kW (1510hp) M-82FN direct-injection engine, which improved its climbing characteristics and manoeuvrability. The modified aircraft, designated La-5FN, made its appearance at the front in March 1943, and played an enormous part in helping the Soviet Air Force establish air superiority for the first time since the German attack on Russia in June 1941.

Lavochkin La-7

Powerplant:	1380kW (1850hp) Ash-82FN radial engine
Performance:	maximum speed 647km/h (402mph) at 5000m (16,405ft); service ceiling 11,000m (36,090ft); range 765km (475 miles)
Weights:	empty 2638kg (5817lb); maximum take-off 3400kg (7496lb)
Dimensions:	wing span 9.80m (32ft 1.33in); length 8.67m (28ft 6in); height 2.54m (8ft 4in)
Armament:	two 20mm (0.79in) or 23mm (0.91in) cannon, plus provision for four 8.20cm (3.23in) rockets or 150kg (330lb) of bombs

Production of the La-5/La-7 series ran to 21,975 aircraft by the end of the war.

An La-7R on a snow-covered airfield.

SOVIET UNION

MIKOYAN-GURYEVICH MIG-1

The MiG-1 was developed to meet a Soviet Air Force requirement, issued in 1938, for a high-altitude fighter, and although it was unstable and difficult to fly it was rushed into production because of its high performance.

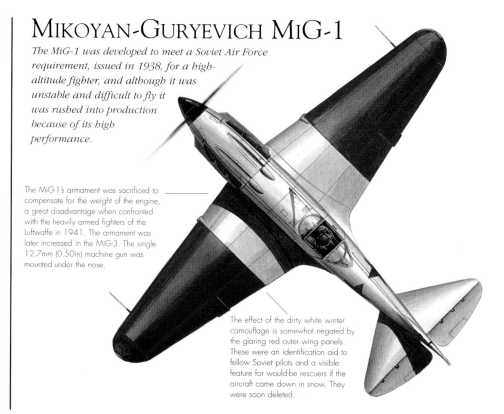

The MiG-1's armament was sacrificed to compensate for the weight of the engine, a great disadvantage when confronted with the heavily armed fighters of the Luftwaffe in 1941. The armament was later increased in the MiG-3. The single 12.7mm (0.50in) machine gun was mounted under the nose.

The effect of the dirty white winter camouflage is somewhat negated by the glaring red outer wing panels. These were an identification aid to fellow Soviet pilots and a visible feature for would-be rescuers if the aircraft came down in snow. They were soon deleted.

Following the tradition of earlier Russian fighters, the MiG-1's pilot sat in an open cockpit, which did not make for comfort at high speeds and high altitudes. The MiG-3 had a fully enclosed cockpit.

Although the MiG-1 had a good performance, it was handicapped by the overall length of the engine, which resulted in poor pitch and directional stability. Although constant attempts were made to improve the MiG series of fighters, they never matched the designs of Yakovlev and Lavochkin.

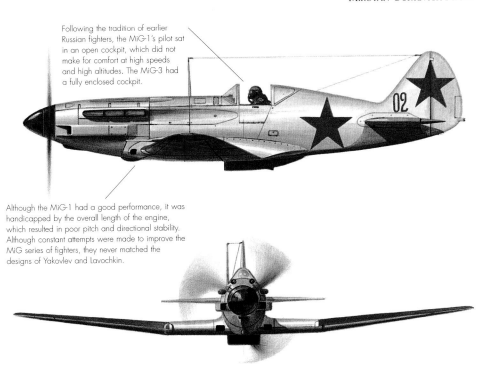

In December 1939 the design bureau of Artem I. Mikoyan and Mikhail I. Guryevich was instructed to construct a single-seat, single-engine monoplane interceptor. The prototype was produced in the record time of four months, and subsequent test flights showed that the aircraft had a high performance.

An updated version of the MiG-1, the MiG-3 featured a fully enclosed cockpit.

Development of the aircraft, which was put into production as the MiG-1, was not without its problems, one of which was that armament had to be sacrificed to compensate for the heavy, high-altitude

Mikulin AM-35A engine that had been specified for the type.

COMPOSITE CONSTRUCTION

The airframe was of composite construction, the front fuselage up to the rear of the cockpit consisting of a steel frame with fabric covering and the rear fuselage of wood. The wing centre-section was of Duralumin, the outer sections of wood.

The MiG-1 was redesignated MiG-3 after the 100th machine had been produced, the main improvements being a fully enclosed cockpit and the addition of an auxiliary fuel tank. Because of the increased combat

Mikoyan-Guryevich MiG-1

Powerplant:	1007kW (1350hp) Mikulin AM-35A 12-cylinder V-type
Performance:	maximum speed 640km/h (398mph) at 5000m (16,405ft); service ceiling 12,000m (39,370ft); range 1195km (742 miles)
Weights:	empty 2595kg (5722lb); maximum take-off 3070kg (6768lb)
Dimensions:	wing span 10.20m (33ft 5.5in); length 8.25m (27ft 0.33in); height 2.65m (8ft 3.25in)
Armament:	one 12.7mm (0.50in) and two 7.62mm (0.30in) machine guns

radius that resulted, MiG-3s were used extensively for fighter reconnaissance.

MiG fighters in formation. MiGs suffered severe losses early in the war.

PETLYAKOV PE-2

Soviet combat aircraft design made massive strides in the early 1940s, and nowhere was this better revealed than in the elegant Petlyakov Pe-2, which performed a multitude of tasks on the Eastern Front.

The aircraft from which the Pe-2 was developed, the VT-100, was originally envisaged as a high-altitude fighter with a pressurized cabin, but it was changed to a dive-bomber, with the cabin de-pressurized and reconfigured for a crew of three. In this guise it emerged as the PB-100.

The third crew member, the radio operator/rear gunner, was installed in a separate compartment to the rear of the fuselage fuel tank. Access was gained through a hatch in the upper fuselage.

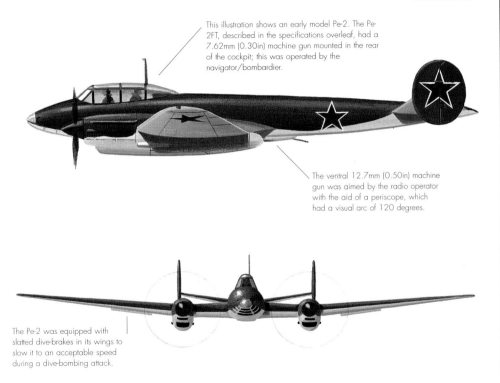

This illustration shows an early model Pe-2. The Pe-2FT, described in the specifications overleaf, had a 7.62mm (0.30in) machine gun mounted in the rear of the cockpit; this was operated by the navigator/bombardier.

The ventral 12.7mm (0.50in) machine gun was aimed by the radio operator with the aid of a periscope, which had a visual arc of 120 degrees.

The Pe-2 was equipped with slatted dive-brakes in its wings to slow it to an acceptable speed during a dive-bombing attack.

Two Petlyakov Pe-2s preparing for take-off on a winter sortie.

Originally designated PB-100 (the PB prefix denoting *Pikiruyushchii Bombardirovshchik*, or dive-bomber), the Pe-2 was ordered into production in February 1941, and over 460 had been delivered at the time of the German invasion in June. A shortage of trained crews meant that comparatively few of these saw action during the early days, and it was not until late August that the Pe-2 was committed to the battle in any numbers, making low-level attacks on German armoured columns. Production of the Pe-2 rapidly got into its stride, a further 1405 aircraft being delivered to operational units in the second half of 1941. Late in 1942 the Pe-2FT appeared, this variant having two 940kW (1260hp) Klimov VK-105PF engines and a 12.7mm (0.50in) UBT machine gun in a dorsal turret, replacing the flexible ShKAS machine gun at the rear of the cockpit. Numerous Pe-2 variants made their appearance during the aircraft's operational career. These included the P2-2M, a prototype with VK-105 engines and an enlarged bomb bay to carry a 500kg (1100lb) bomb; the Pe-2FZ, a variant of the Pe-2FT with better cabin facilities; the Pe-2I, which had a mid- instead of a low-wing configuration; and the Pe-2UT dual-control trainer. Total production of the Pe-2/3, all variants, was 11,427 aircraft.

Petlyakov Pe-2FT

Powerplant: two 940kW (1260hp) Klimov VK-105PF 12-cylinder V-type

Performance: maximum speed 580km/h (360mph) at 4000m (13,125ft); service ceiling 8800m (28,870 ft); range 1315km (817 miles) with a 1000kg (2205lb) bomb load

Weights: empty 5950kg (13,119lb); maximum take-off 8520kg (18,783lb) loaded

Dimensions: wing span 17.11m (56ft 1.33in); length 12.78m (41ft 11in); height 3.42m (11ft 2.5in)

Armament: six 7.62mm (0.30in) or 12.7mm (0.50in) machine guns; 1600kg (3527lb) of bombs

The Pe-2 was an excellent tactical bomber, comparable with the Mosquito.

PETLYAKOV PE-8

*Like the Luftwaffe and the Italian Air Force, the
Soviet Air Force in WWII was geared to tactical
support, and paid little attention to strategic bombers.*

Use of the Pe-8 was restricted
because of a shortage of
AM-35A engines. In 1943,
when the situation had become
critical, I.F. Nezval, who had
taken over the Pe-8 programme
after Petlyakov's death,
redesigned it to take the
M-82FN.

This Pe-8 of the Soviet Long-
Range Aviation is
camouflaged in the
standard pattern of dark
green upper surfaces and
pale blue under surfaces.
Apart from the application
of temporary winter
camouflage, this was
retained throughout the war.

An unusual feature of the Pe-8 was that it had machine gun positions built into the rear of the two inboard engine nacelles. Gunners found these positions cramped and smelly, but they had the advantage of being warm. They were deleted in the later production version.

The Pe-8's bomb bay could accommodate a 5000kg (11023lb) FAB-5000NG blast bomb. On the eve of the Battle of Kursk in July 1943, Pe-8s were used to drop these weapons on concentrations of German tanks and other armoured vehicles.

SOVIET UNION

139

The Pe-8 was the only Soviet strategic heavy bomber to see service in WWII. Design work began in 1934, the type originally bearing the designation ANT-42, which indicated that it was a product of the Andrei N. Tupolev design bureau. However, at the end of 1940 credit was given to Vladimir Petlyakov, who had

This Pe-8 brought Soviet Foreign Minister Molotov on a visit to Britain in 1942.

led the team responsible for the bomber's design, and the designation Pe-8 was adopted. First flown on 27 December 1936, the Pe-8 entered service in 1940, and in the summer of 1941 carried out the first major strategic attack of the war when a small force of bombers raided Berlin.

ENGINE DIFFICULTIES

The Pe-8 was dogged by engine difficulties throughout its career and various powerplants were tried, including M-30B diesel engines. From 1943, production Pe-8s were fitted with Mikulin M-82FN fuel injection engines, but the problems persisted and production ended in 1944 after 79 examples had been built. Despite its troubles, the Pe-8 made some notable long-distance flights, including one of more than 17,700km (11,000 miles) from Moscow to Washington and back via Scotland, Iceland and Canada.

Petlyakov Pe-8 (ANT-42)

Powerplant:	four 1007kW (1350hp) Mikulin AM-35A V-type
Performance:	maximum speed 438km/h (272mph) at 7600m (24,935ft); service ceiling 9750m (31,988ft); range 5445km (3383 miles)
Weights:	empty 18,420kg (40,616lb); maximum take-off 33,325kg (73,481lb)
Dimensions:	wing span 39.94m (131ft 0.25in); length 22.47m (73ft 8.5in); height 6.10m (20ft)
Armament:	one 20mm (0.79in) cannon; one 12.7mm (0.50in) machine gun and two 7.62mm (0.30in) machine guns; bomb load of up to 4000kg (8820lb)

The Pe-8 was Russia's only modern four-engined strategic bomber.

POLIKARPOV I-153

In the 1930s the Soviet designer Nikolai N. Polikarpov was at the forefront of Soviet fighter design, and at the outbreak of the war in the east it was aircraft of his design that were the mainstay of the Soviet Air Force's fighter squadrons.

The I-153's progenitor, the I-15, had featured a gull-type upper wing, whereas the next variant, the I-15bis (I-152), was fitted with a straight wing. The I-153 reverted to the gull-wing arrangement; its manoeuvrability surpassed that of all other contemporary biplanes.

The I-153 pilot sat in an open cockpit, with only a small windscreen for protection.

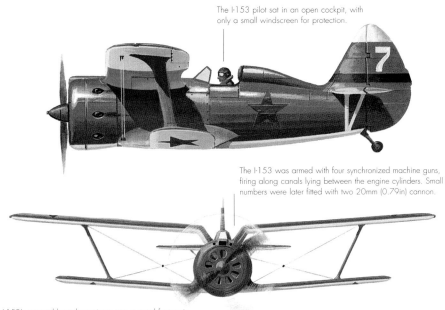

The I-153 was armed with four synchronized machine guns, firing along canals lying between the engine cylinders. Small numbers were later fitted with two 20mm (0.79in) cannon.

The I-153's retractable undercarriage was a novel feature in a biplane. Both legs retracted rearward into the underside of the fuselage, the wheels being turned 90 degrees during the process until they lay flat. As with many other Soviet aircraft, there was provision to fit skis instead of wheels.

SOVIET UNION

First flown in 1938, the Polikarpov I-153 was developed from the I-15 fighter biplane. Unlike its predecessor it featured a retractable undercarriage, but the maximum speed of the early I-153s 386km/h (240mp/h) was still insufficient when compared with that of the new monoplane fighter aircraft which were beginning to

The I-15, pictured here at Moscow Park, was a highly manoeuvrable aircraft.

enter service with the principal European air forces. The M-25V engine was later replaced by an M-62R developing 746kW (1000hp), and then by a 820kW (1100hp) M-63, which raised the I-153's speed to its ultimate of

426km/h (265mph). The I-153, dubbed *Chaika* (Seagull) because of its distinctive wing shape, was a first-rate combat aircraft and was subsequently to prove its worth in air fighting, being able to out-turn almost every aircraft that opposed it in action. The I-153 saw its first action in the 1939 Sino-Soviet incident, and was heavily involved in the 'Winter War' between Russia and Finland in 1939–40. The type was quickly withdrawn from first-line Soviet AF units after the German invasion of the USSR, but the Finns were still using captured I-153s as first-line fighters up to 1944. The *Chaika* was the last

Polikarpov I-153 Chaika

Powerplant:	746kW (1000hp) Shvetsov M-62 9-cylinder radial
Performance:	max speed 444km/h (276mph) at 3000m (9845ft); service ceiling 10,700m (35,105ft); range: 880km (547 miles)
Weights:	empty 1348kg (2972lb); maximum take-off 2110kg (4652lb)
Dimensions:	wing span 10.00m (32ft 9.5in); length 6.17m (20ft 3in); height 2.80m (9ft 2.25in)
Armament:	four 7.62mm (0.30in) machine guns, plus a light bomb load or six air-to-ground rockets

single-seat fighter biplane to be series-produced in the Soviet Union.

An I-153 fighter on an airstrip in the Crimea in the late summer of 1941.

SOVIET UNION

145

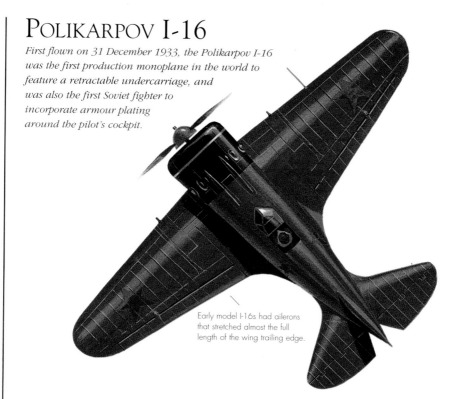

POLIKARPOV I-16

First flown on 31 December 1933, the Polikarpov I-16 was the first production monoplane in the world to feature a retractable undercarriage, and was also the first Soviet fighter to incorporate armour plating around the pilot's cockpit.

Early model I-16s had ailerons that stretched almost the full length of the wing trailing edge.

The I-16 was a tricky aircraft to fly. The front section of the fuselage, with the engine, was too close to the centre of gravity, and the pilot's cockpit was located too far to the rear. There was insufficient longitudinal stability and it was impossible to fly the aircraft 'hands off'.

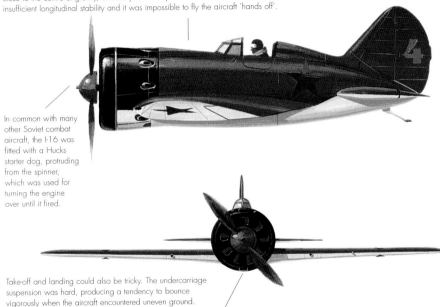

In common with many other Soviet combat aircraft, the I-16 was fitted with a Hucks starter dog, protruding from the spinner, which was used for turning the engine over until it fired.

Take-off and landing could also be tricky. The undercarriage suspension was hard, producing a tendency to bounce vigorously when the aircraft encountered uneven ground. Undercarriage retraction also caused problems; the pilot had to turn a hand crank 44 times before retraction was complete.

SOVIET UNION

147

During the mid-1930s, the basic I-16 design was progressively modified to carry out a variety of different tasks. Among the variants produced was the TsKB-18, an assault version armed with four PV-1 synchronized machine guns, two wing-mounted machine guns and 100kg (220lb) of bombs. The pilot was protected by

The Polikarpov I-16 was unstable, difficult to fly and had poor visibility.

armour plating in front, below and behind. In 1938 the I-16 Type 17 was tested, armed with two wing-mounted cannon. This version was produced in large numbers. Then, with the cooperation of the armament engineer B.G. Shpitalnii, Polikarpov produced the TsKB-12P, the first aircraft in the world to be armed with two synchronized cannon firing through the propeller arc. The last fighter version of the I-16 was the Type 24, fitted with a 746kW (1000hp) M-62R engine which gave it a top speed of 523km/h (325mph). Altogether, 6555 I-16s were built before production ended in 1940. I-16s fought in Spain, against the Japanese in the Far East, and against the Luftwaffe. The type's short, stubby fuselage created handling problems, but in the hands of an experienced pilot the I-16 was a highly manoeuvrable and worthy opponent.

Polikarpov I-16

Powerplant:	820kW (1100hp) Shvetsov M-63 9-cylinder radial
Performance:	maximum speed: 489km/h (304mph) at 3000m (9845ft); service ceiling 9000m (29,530ft); range: 700km (435 miles)
Weights:	empty 1490kg (3285lb); maximum take-off 2095kg (4619lb)
Dimensions:	wing span 9.00m (29ft 6.25in); length 6.13m (20ft 1.25in); height 2.57m (8ft 5in)
Armament:	four 7.62mm (0.30in) machine guns or two 7.62mm (0.30in) machine guns and two 20mm (0.79in) cannon; external bomb and rocket load of 500kg (1102lb)

ЗаСталина!

This I-16 carries the slogan 'For Stalin' on its fuselage side.

TUPOLEV SB-2

The Tupolev SB-2 was almost certainly the most capable light bomber in service anywhere in the world in the mid-1930s. It was the first aircraft of modern stressed-skin construction to be produced in the USSR, and in numerical terms was also the most important bomber of its day.

The SB-2's broad, high aspect ratio wing gave it a good altitude performance of nearly 9150m (30,000ft). Russian crews nicknamed the bomber the 'Pterodactyl'.

The SB-2 was used operationally in Spain, where its crews held it in great esteem and gave it the nickname 'Katushka'. It was considered to be invulnerable, as it was faster than most fighters then in service.

There were a number of foreign customers for the SB-2. They were mostly happy with the aircraft's performance, but there were complaints about the high noise level, cramped crew compartments, hard undercarriage suspension and in particular about the front gunner's position. This could only be reached through a hatch under the fuselage, so he had no means of escape in the event of a belly landing or a ditching.

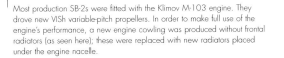

Most production SB-2s were fitted with the Klimov M-103 engine. They drove new VISh variable-pitch propellers. In order to make full use of the engine's performance, a new engine cowling was produced without frontal radiators (as seen here); these were replaced with new radiators placed under the engine nacelle.

SOVIET UNION

The story of the SB-2 (the initials stand for *Skorostnoy Bombardirovshchik*, or high speed bomber) began in the early 1930s, when Andrei N. Tupolev embarked on design studies of a fast tactical bomber. Considering the official requirement to be inadequate, he built two prototypes according to the Air Force

The SB-2 saw action in the Spanish Civil War and in the 'Winter War'.

Technical Office specification, and a third according to his own. All three prototypes, designated ANT-40, ANT-40-1 and ANT-40-2, flew in 1934, and Tupolev's own version, the ANT-40-2, proved the best. The type was ordered into production, entering service in 1936, and 6967 aircraft were built before production ended in 1941. The type saw action in the Spanish Civil War and in the 'Winter War' against Finland in 1939–40. Among the principal variants were the SB-2bis of 1938, with uprated engines and greater fuel capacity, and the SB-2RK dive-bomber version of 1940. By the time of the German invasion of Russia in 1941 the SB-2 was obsolescent, and heavy losses sustained in daylight attacks led to the aircraft being switched to night bombing. Later, many SB-2s were used as target tugs, crew trainers and transports. The bomber was licence-built in Czechoslovakia as the B-71, 111 being produced. The SB-3 was an improved

Tupolev SB-2bis

Powerplant:	two 716kW (960hp) Klimov M-103 12-cylinder V-type
Performance:	maximum speed 450km/h (280mph) at 1000m (3281ft); service ceiling 9000m (29,530ft); range 2300km (1429 miles)
Weights:	empty 4768kg (10,511lb); maximum take-off 7880kg (17,372lb)
Dimensions:	wing span 20.33m (66ft 8.5in); length 12.57m (41ft 2.33in); height 3.25m (10ft 8in)
Armament:	four 7.62mm (0.30in) machine guns; bomb load of 600kg (1323lb)

version with M-103A engines, and was first produced in 1937.

An SB-2 in winter camouflage. The type suffered appalling losses in 1941.

TUPOLEV TU-2

The Tupolev Tu-2 was one of the outstanding combat aircraft of World War II, and although it did not enter service until 1944, it played a key part in the Red Army's final offensives.

After World War II, the Tu-2 proved to be an ideal test vehicle for various powerplants, including the first generation of Soviet jet engines. Production continued after 1945, some 3000 aircraft eventually being delivered to various Soviet Bloc air forces. The last Tu-2 model was the ANT-68, a high-altitude version that saw limited service as the Tu-10.

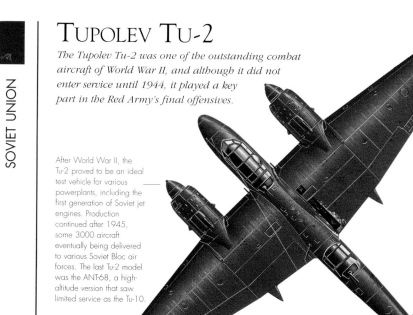

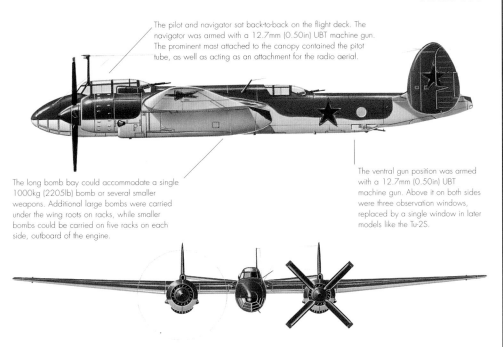

The pilot and navigator sat back-to-back on the flight deck. The navigator was armed with a 12.7mm (0.50in) UBT machine gun. The prominent mast attached to the canopy contained the pitot tube, as well as acting as an attachment for the radio aerial.

The long bomb bay could accommodate a single 1000kg (2205lb) bomb or several smaller weapons. Additional large bombs were carried under the wing roots on racks, while smaller bombs could be carried on five racks on each side, outboard of the engine.

The ventral gun position was armed with a 12.7mm (0.50in) UBT machine gun. Above it on both sides were three observation windows, replaced by a single window in later models like the Tu-2S.

SOVIET UNION

155

The prototype Tu-2 (ANT-58) flew for the first time on 29 January 1941 and subsequent flight testing showed that the aircraft had an outstanding performance. Because of shortages, it was decided to replace the intended Mikulin AM-37 engines with Shvetsov Ash-82 radials. But because of technical problems series

Late production Tu-2s, like this example, featured numerous modifications.

production of the Tu-2 did not start until 1943, and combat units did not begin to rearm with the bomber until the spring of 1944. Although total wartime production was only 1111 aircraft, the Tu-2 proved to be of immense value to the Soviet tactical bomber forces, and also saw service in a number of other roles. One of these was as a carrier for the GAZ-67B cross-country vehicle, which was widely used by Soviet paratroop units. The vehicle was carried partially recessed in the aircraft's bomb bay and dropped by parachute.

LONG-RANGE AND ATTACK VARIANTS

In October 1944 a long-range variant, the Tu-2D (ANT-62), made its appearance; this had an increased span and a crew of five. A torpedo-bomber variant, the Tu-2T (ANT-62T), was tested between January and March 1945 and issued to Soviet Naval Aviation units. The Tu-2R, also designated Tu-6, carried a battery of cameras in the bomb bay. An experimental ground-attack version, the Tu-2Sh, was tested with various armament combinations; these included a 75mm (2.95in) gun mounted in a 'solid' nose, and a battery of 48 7.62mm (0.30in)

sub-machine guns mounted in the bomb bay, directed to fire downwards on unprotected personnel.

Tupolev Tu-2S

Powerplant:	two 1380kW (1850hp) Shvetsov Ash-82FN radial engines
Performance:	maximum speed 547km/h (340mph) at 5400m (17,716ft); service ceiling: 9500m (31,170ft); range 2000km (1243 miles)
Weights:	empty 7474kg (16,477lb); maximum take-off 12,800kg (28,219lb)
Dimensions:	wing span 18.86m (61ft 10.5 in); length 13.80m (45ft 3.33in); height 4.56m (14ft 11in)
Armament:	two 20mm (0.79in) cannon and three 12.7mm (0.50in) machine guns, plus a maximum bomb load of 3000kg (6614lb)

YAKOVLEV YAK-1

The Russians were late in developing really effective monoplane fighters that were in the same class as Britain's Hurricane and Spitfire and Germany's Bf 109, but Aleksandr Yakovlev's attractive designs soon redressed the situation.

The standard armament of the Yak-1 was a pair of 12.7mm (0.50in) machine guns in the upper front fuselage, and a 20mm (0.79in) ShVAK cannon in the nose, firing through the propeller boss, with 120 rounds of ammunition. A version of the Yak-3, the Yak-3K, was armed with a 45mm (1.77in) cannon, while the Yak-3T had a 37mm (1.45in) weapon.

The Yak-1's radiator was mounted under the fuselage. Excess air was dumped through an ejector flap in the rear of the radiator fairing, which could be closed if not required.

The Yak-1 had a four-piece cockpit canopy, which gave the pilot poor
visibility. Cockpit equipment was rudimentary; the gunsight was primitive,
there were no blind flying instruments, and no fuel gauges.

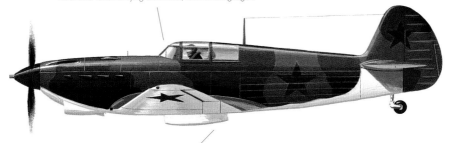

The airframe of the Yak-1 was lightweight, giving rise to a
generation of fast and manoeuvrable interceptors; on the
other hand, the more robust Yak-7A was developed into a
succession of heavier tactical fighters like the Yak-9.

SOVIET UNION

159

The Yak-1 *Krasavyets* (Beauty) made its first public appearance at an air display on 7 November 1940. It was Aleksandr S. Yakovlev's first fighter design, and it earned him the Order of Lenin, the gift of a Zis car and a prize of 100,000 roubles. The fighter was powered by a 746kW (1000hp) M-105PA engine and carried an

Yak-1 fighters being rolled out of the assembly shop of an aircraft factory.

armament of one 20mm (0.79in) ShVAK cannon, two 7.62mm (0.30in) ShKAS machine guns and sometimes six RS-82 rockets. The Yak-1 was of mixed construction, fabric and plywood covered; it was simple to build and service, and a delight to fly. Maximum speed was 500km/h (310mph). Production was slow because of the relocation of factories after the German invasion, and so it was decided to convert a trainer variant of the Yak-1, the Yak-7V, into a single-seat fighter by covering the second cockpit with metal sheeting. In this new guise the aircraft was designated Yak-7A. In 1942 the basic Yak-1 evolved into the Yak-1M, which had a smaller wing area, a revised rear fuselage and a three-piece sliding cockpit hood; it was also slightly faster than the Yak-1. Similar modifications to the Yak-7A led to the improved Yak-7B, of which 6399 were built. Further refinements to the Yak-1M were introduced before the

Yakovlev-1

Powerplant:	820kW (1100hp) VK-105 12-cylinder Vee-type engine
Performance:	maximum speed 600km/h (373mph) at 3500m (11,482ft); service ceiling 10,000m (32,810ft); range 700km (435 miles)
Weights:	empty 2347kg (5174lb); maximum take-off 2660kg (5863lb)
Dimensions:	wing span 9.20m (30ft 2in); length 8.55m (28ft 0in); height 3.00m (9ft 10in)
Armament:	one 20mm (0.79in) cannon and two 12.7mm (0.50in) machine guns

aircraft entered quantity production in the spring of 1943, the resulting fighter being redesignated Yak-3.

This Yak-1B carries a message to its pilot from his collective worker comrades.

AVRO LANCASTER B.MK.I (SPECIAL)

*In August 1943 No 617 (Dam Busters) Squadron
began to receive Lancaster Mk Is specially modified to
carry the Tallboy penetration bomb. Later, further
modifications enabled the aircraft to carry the
ten-ton Grand Slam, seen here.*

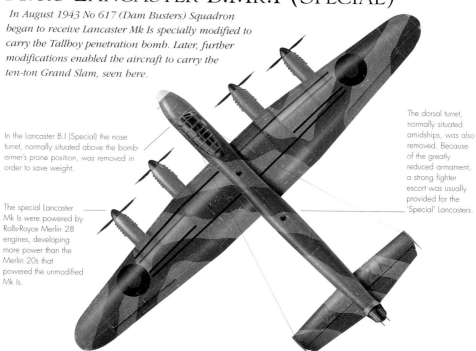

In the Lancaster B.I (Special) the nose
turret, normally situated above the bomb-
aimer's prone position, was removed in
order to save weight.

The special Lancaster
Mk Is were powered by
Rolls-Royce Merlin 28
engines, developing
more power than the
Merlin 20s that
powered the unmodified
Mk Is.

The dorsal turret,
normally situated
amidships, was also
removed. Because
of the greatly
reduced armament,
a strong fighter
escort was usually
provided for the
'Special' Lancasters.

From this astrodome, just behind the main cockpit area, the navigator could fix his position by taking 'star shots' with a sextant.

As a weight-saving measure, the normal tail armament of four machine guns was reduced to two in the hydraulically operated Frazer-Nash gun turret.

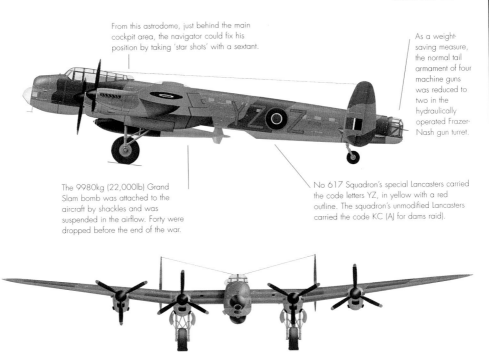

The 9980kg (22,000lb) Grand Slam bomb was attached to the aircraft by shackles and was suspended in the airflow. Forty were dropped before the end of the war.

No 617 Squadron's special Lancasters carried the code letters YZ, in yellow with a red outline. The squadron's unmodified Lancasters carried the code KC (AJ for dams raid).

Deployment of the Lancaster B.Mk.I (Special) provided proof of this famous bomber's amazing development potential. The prototype Lancaster B.I flew on 9 January 1941, and the first operational sortie with Lancasters was on 3 March 1942, when four aircraft laid mines in the Heligoland Bight. Little

The Battle of Britain Memorial Flight's Lancaster B.III, PA474.

modification was made during its life to the basic Lancaster airframe, although 'special' aircraft (Mk IIIs) issued to No 617 squadron prior to its famous attack on the Ruhr dams in May 1943 had a 'cut-out' bomb bay to accommodate the Barnes Wallis mine (popularly known as the 'bouncing bomb') used in that operation.

OPERATIONAL USE

Using its specially modified Lancaster Is, No 617 Squadron carried out an attack on the Dortmund-Ems Canal on the night of 15/16 September 1943, marking the first operational use of the 5443kg (12,000lb) Tallboy bomb. Later, specially strengthened deep-penetration variants of this weapon were used against 'hardened' targets like U-boat pens. The first operational use of the 9980kg (22,000lb) Grand Slam bomb was on 14 March 1945, against the Bielefeld viaduct. Thirty-three Lancaster B.Mk.I Specials were produced in total.

Lancaster B.Mk.I (Special)

Powerplant:	four 1223kW (1640hp) Rolls-Royce Merlin 28 or 38 12-cylinder V-type engines
Performance:	Maximum speed 462km/h (287mph) at 4000m (13,125ft); service ceiling 5790m (19,000ft); range 2784km (1730 miles) with maximum bomb load
Weights:	empty 16,738kg (36,900lb); maximum take-off 31,751kg (70,000lb)
Dimensions:	wing span 31.09m (102ft); length 21.18m (69ft 6in); height 6.25m (20ft 6in)
Armament:	two 7.7mm (0.303in) machine guns plus 5443kg (12,000lb) bomb load

UNITED KINGDOM

Lancaster Mk I QB-P of No 424 Squadron RCAF.

165

AVRO MANCHESTER MK I

The Manchester pictured here served with No 83 Squadron at RAF Scampton, Lincolnshire, in March 1942. The aircraft failed to return from its 15th operational sortie to Hamburg.

Early trials with the Manchester revealed that when the nose turret was rotated, the airflow along the fuselage sides was disturbed. The problem was solved by moving the turret's axis of rotation slightly forward.

Among the modifications made to the Manchester as a result of flight trials was an extension of the wing span by 3.05m (10ft).

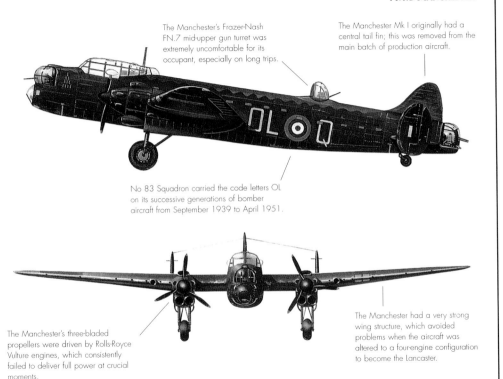

The Manchester's Frazer-Nash FN.7 mid-upper gun turret was extremely uncomfortable for its occupant, especially on long trips.

The Manchester Mk I originally had a central tail fin; this was removed from the main batch of production aircraft.

No 83 Squadron carried the code letters OL on its successive generations of bomber aircraft from September 1939 to April 1951.

The Manchester's three-bladed propellers were driven by Rolls-Royce Vulture engines, which consistently failed to deliver full power at crucial moments.

The Manchester had a very strong wing structure, which avoided problems when the aircraft was altered to a four-engine configuration to become the Lancaster.

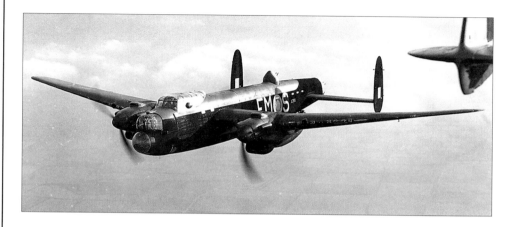

The Avro Manchester was designed to meet British Air Ministry Specification 13/36, which called for a twin-engined heavy bomber. The airframe design was good, but the engines selected to power the bomber were 1312kW (1760hp) Rolls-Royce Vultures, a choice dictated by the need to conserve Merlin engines for the

An Avro Manchester in flight.

RAF's Hurricane and Spitfire fighters. The prototype Manchester flew on 25 July 1939, followed by a second aircraft on 26 May 1940. The Manchester Mk I, which featured a central tail fin as well as twin fins and rudders, went operational with No 207

Squadron in November 1940. The first 20 aircraft were followed by 200 Manchester IAs with the central fin removed.

UNRELIABLE ENGINES

The Manchester carried out its first operational sortie, an attack on Brest harbour, on the night of 24/25 February 1941. Six aircraft of No 207 Squadron formed part of the attacking force. The bomber was withdrawn from operations in 1942. Its unreliable engines, which were prone to catching fire without warning, had cost the lives of many aircrew and resulted in a loss rate of 40% on operations and 25% on training flights. The Manchester Mk III, modified to take four Rolls-Royce Merlin

engines, became the prototype Avro Lancaster.

Avro Manchester Mk I

Powerplant:	two 1312kW (1760hp) Rolls-Royce Vulture 24-cylinder X-type engines
Performance:	max speed 426km/h (265mph) at 5180m (17,000ft); service ceiling 5850m (19,200ft); max range 2623km (1630 miles)
Weights:	empty 13,350kg (29,432lb); maximum take-off 22,680kg (50,000lb)
Dimensions:	wing span 27.46m (90ft 1in); length 21.14m (69ft 4.25in); height 5.94m (19ft 6in)
Armament:	eight 7.7mm (0.303in) machine guns, plus internal bomb load of 4695kg (10,350lb)

Manchester EM-U of No 207 Squadron.

BRISTOL BEAUFIGHTER TF.MK X

*The Beaufighter TF.Mk X pictured here served with
No 489 Squadron, RNZAF, which was part of the
Coastal Command Strike Wing based at
Dallachy, Scotland.*

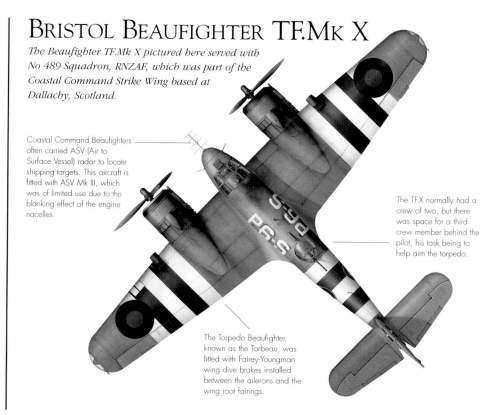

Coastal Command Beaufighters often carried ASV (Air to Surface Vessel) radar to locate shipping targets. This aircraft is fitted with ASV Mk III, which was of limited use due to the blanking effect of the engine nacelles.

The TF.X normally had a crew of two, but there was space for a third crew member behind the pilot, his task being to help aim the torpedo.

The Torpedo Beaufighter, known as the Torbeau, was fitted with Fairey-Youngman wing dive brakes installed between the ailerons and the wing root fairings.

The code P6 was used by No 489 Squadron's Beaufighters from December 1943 to August 1945. Prior to that, the code XA was used on the squadron's Handley Page Hampdens.

This No 489 Squadron Torbeau is depicted with 'invasion stripes' over the standard Coastal Command scheme of dark sea grey over grey. Most Torbeau operations were directed against German convoys off Norway.

UNITED KINGDOM

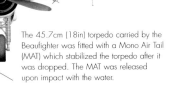

The 45.7cm (18in) torpedo carried by the Beaufighter was fitted with a Mono Air Tail (MAT) which stabilized the torpedo after it was dropped. The MAT was released upon impact with the water.

UNITED KINGDOM

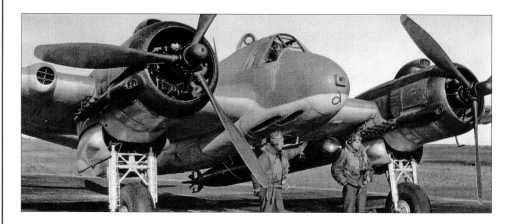

Although the Bristol Beaufighter's main claim to fame was as a night fighter, it was also developed as a long-range strike fighter for RAF Coastal Command. The first strike fighter variant was the Beaufighter Mk IC, 300 of which were produced. It was supplanted by the Mk VI (the Mks III, IV and V being

A Beaufighter TF. Mk. X of a Coastal Command Strike Wing, and crew.

experimental aircraft). Mk VIs for Fighter Command were designated Mk VIF (879 aircraft), and those for Coastal Command Mk VIC (693 aircraft). Sixty Mk VIs on the production line were completed as Interim

Torpedo Fighters, but two new variants for Coastal Command soon appeared. These were the TF. Mk X torpedo-bomber and the Mk XIC, which was not equipped to carry torpedoes. Both were fitted with 1320kW (1770hp) Hercules XVII engines and had a dorsal cupola containing a rearward-firing 7.7mm (0.303in) machine gun. Production of the TF. Mk X, which was the most important British anti-shipping aircraft from 1944 to the end of the war, totalled 2205 aircraft, while 163 aircraft were completed to Mk XIC standard. The Beaufighter TF. Mk X was also built in Australia as the TF. Mk 21 (364 aircraft), the RAAF using it to good effect in the south-west Pacific.

Beaufighter TF.Mk X

Powerplant:	two 1320kW (1770hp) Hercules XVII 14-cylinder radials
Performance:	max speed 512km/h (318mph); service ceiling 4572m (15,000ft); range 2366km (1470 miles)
Weights:	empty 7076kg (15,600lb); maximum take-off 11,431kg (25,200lb)
Dimensions:	wing span 17.63m (57ft 10in); length 12.70m (41ft 8in); height 4.82m (15ft 10in)
Armament:	four 20mm (0.79in) cannon and one 7.7mm (0.303in) machine gun; one 748kg (1650lb) or 965kg (2127lb) torpedo, two 227kg (500lb) bombs, eight 76.2mm (3in) rocket projectiles.

The Beaufighter TF. Mk X was derived from the Mk I night fighter, seen here.

BRISTOL BLENHEIM MK IV

The Blenheim Mk IV shown here is an aircraft of No 59 Squadron, which operated from Poix as part of the British Expeditionary Force's Air Component in France during the spring of 1940.

The Blenheim's Bristol Mercury engines had a prominent intake projecting forward from the engine cowling. These were ram air intakes for the oil cooler.

Only a small proportion of the Blenheim's vertical tail surfaces was fixed, the aircraft having a large full-height rudder controlled by cables running the length of the fuselage.

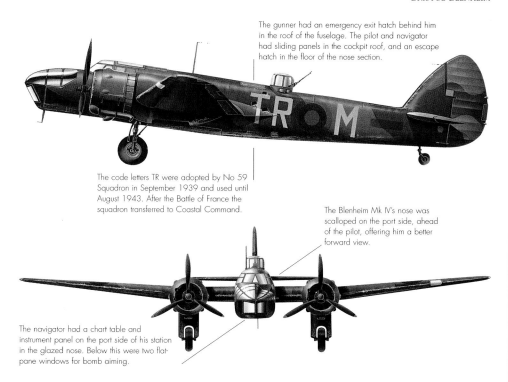

The gunner had an emergency exit hatch behind him in the roof of the fuselage. The pilot and navigator had sliding panels in the cockpit roof, and an escape hatch in the floor of the nose section.

The code letters TR were adopted by No 59 Squadron in September 1939 and used until August 1943. After the Battle of France the squadron transferred to Coastal Command.

The Blenheim Mk IV's nose was scalloped on the port side, ahead of the pilot, offering him a better forward view.

The navigator had a chart table and instrument panel on the port side of his station in the glazed nose. Below this were two flat-pane windows for bomb aiming.

UNITED KINGDOM

In September 1935 the Air Ministry placed an initial order for 150 Bristol Blenheim Mk Is, a design developed from an eight-seat fast passenger aircraft. A second order for 434 aircraft followed in December 1936. 1280 Mk Is were built in total, and of these 1007 were serving with the RAF at the outbreak of war in September

This lovingly restored Blenheim Mk IV is in the markings of No 254 Squadron.

1939, including 147 Blenheim Mk IF fighters.

REARMED

By that time, however, the home-based squadrons had rearmed with the improved

Blenheim Mk IV, which was basically a Mk I airframe with two 674kW (905hp) Mercury XV radials driving de Havilland three-blade variable pitch propellers, extra fuel tankage and a redesigned, lengthened nose. On the second day of the war aircraft of Nos 107 and 110 Squadrons from Marham, Norfolk, carried out the RAF's first offensive operation when they unsuccessfully attacked units of the German Navy in the Elbe Estuary. The total inadequacy of the Blenheim's defensive armament became apparent in the battles of Norway and France, when the Blenheim squadrons engaged in anti-shipping operations in the North Sea and those

Bristol Blenheim Mk IV

Powerplant:	two 674kW (905hp) Bristol Mercury XV radial engines
Performance:	max speed 428km/h (266mph) at 3595m (11,800ft); service ceiling 6705m (22,000ft); range 2340km (1460 miles)
Weights:	empty 4441kg (9790lb); maximum take-off 6537kg (14,400lb)
Dimensions:	wing span 17.70m (58ft 1in); length 12.98m (42ft 7in); height 2.99m (9ft 10in)
Armament:	five 7.7mm (0.303in) machine guns; internal bomb load of 454kg (1000lb)

deployed to France suffered appalling losses.

A Bristol Blenheim Mk IV of No 13 Operational Training Unit.

177

de Havilland Mosquito PR.Mk.XVI

The Mosquito PR.Mk.XVI RF992/R illustrated here belongs to the 654th Bomb Squadron, 25th Bomb Group (Reconnaissance), 325th Photo Wing, based at RAF Watton, Norfolk, in March 1945.

One of the Mosquito's major recognition features was its distinctive wing planform, with engine nacelles extending forward of the fuselage nose.

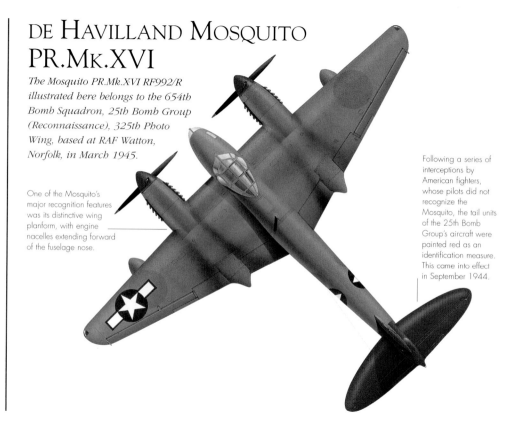

Following a series of interceptions by American fighters, whose pilots did not recognize the Mosquito, the tail units of the 25th Bomb Group's aircraft were painted red as an identification measure. This came into effect in September 1944.

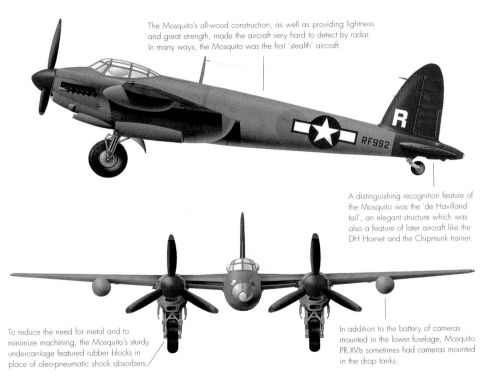

The Mosquito's all-wood construction, as well as providing lightness and great strength, made the aircraft very hard to detect by radar. In many ways, the Mosquito was the first 'stealth' aircraft.

A distinguishing recognition feature of the Mosquito was the 'de Havilland tail', an elegant structure which was also a feature of later aircraft like the DH Hornet and the Chipmunk trainer.

To reduce the need for metal and to minimize machining, the Mosquito's sturdy undercarriage featured rubber blocks in place of oleo-pneumatic shock absorbers.

In addition to the battery of cameras mounted in the lower fuselage, Mosquito PR.XVIs sometimes had cameras mounted in the drop tanks.

UNITED KINGDOM

179

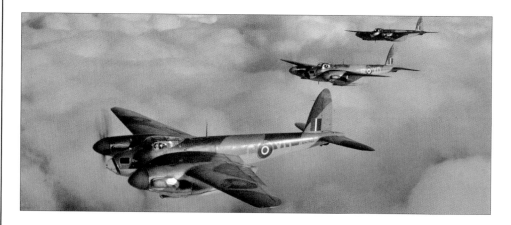

First flown in July 1943, the Mosquito PR.Mk.XVI was a high-altitude photo-reconnaissance variant of the famous de Havilland warplane with two-stage Merlins and a pressurized cabin. One aircraft, NS729, was fitted with deck landing gear. Production of the PR.Mk.XVI ran to 402 aircraft, of which only six were lost on

Mosquitoes of No 105 Squadron, the first Mosquito bomber unit.

operations. About 80 PR.XVIs were issued to the USAAF, and in September 1944 aircraft of the the 654th Reconnaissance Squadron of the 25th Bomb Group, USAAF, were assigned to reconnaissance and air control operations in the Arnhem-Nijmegen area from the start of the Allied airborne landings there.

ARNHEM BRIDGE

Bad weather made regular air reconnaissance impossible, so the 654th Squadron was ordered to despatch a Mosquito to the Arnhem bridge every hour, on the hour, in the hope of finding a clear patch through which to take photographs, or at least make a visual observation. This they did, at great risk to the crews, until it was established that the bridge was in enemy hands. The Mosquito PR.XVI also equipped several RAF squadrons, some of which operated in the Far East in the closing

Mosquito PR.Mk.XVI

Powerplant:	two 1275kW (1710hp) Rolls-Royce Merlin 76 or 77 Vee-type
Performance:	maximum speed 667km/h (415mph); service ceiling 11,742m (38,500ft); range 3942km (2450 miles)
Weights:	empty 6630kg (14,619lb); maximum take-off 10,419kg (23,000lb)
Dimensions:	wing span 16.53m (54ft 2in); length 13.57m (44ft 6in); height 3.80m (12ft 5.5in)
Armament:	none

stages of the war. The Mosquito PR.Mk.34, which entered service in June 1945, was a very long range version of the Pr.XVI.

Mosquito PR.34 VL618 is seen here in the markings of South-East Asia Command.

FAIREY SWORDFISH

Affectionately known as the 'Stringbag', the Fairey Swordfish made a decisive contribution to the war, especially in the Mediterranean. The biplane torpedo-bomber served in all theatres.

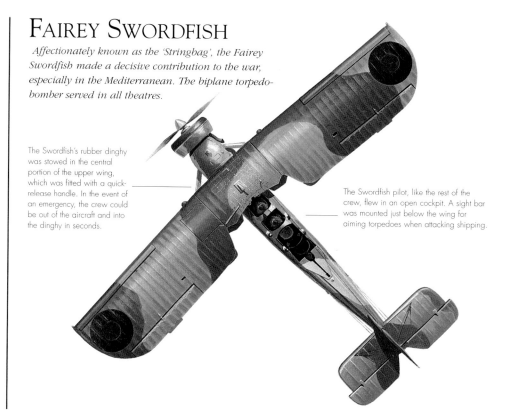

The Swordfish's rubber dinghy was stowed in the central portion of the upper wing, which was fitted with a quick-release handle. In the event of an emergency, the crew could be out of the aircraft and into the dinghy in seconds.

The Swordfish pilot, like the rest of the crew, flew in an open cockpit. A sight bar was mounted just below the wing for aiming torpedoes when attacking shipping.

Primary armament of the Swordfish was the 457mm (18in) torpedo. In May 1941, this weapon crippled the mighty German battleship *Bismarck*, enabling warships to close in and finish her off.

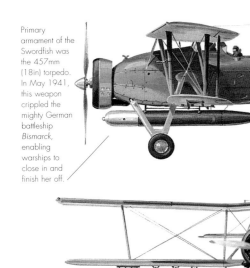

The arrester hook, retracted here, was a vital part of the aircraft's fittings for service on carriers, The Swordfish's wings were also hinged to fold back against the fuselage to reduce the amount of stowage space needed by each aircraft.

The Swordfish Mk III could carry eight rocket projectiles, four under each wing. Two German U-boats were sunk by Swordfish rocket attack, and the rockets were used against many other vessels in the closing months of the war.

Flown for the first time on 17 April 1934, the first Swordfish Mk Is were delivered to No 825 Squadron of the Fleet Air Arm in July 1936. By the outbreak of World War II 689 Swordfish had been delivered or were on order. Thirteen squadrons were equipped with the aircraft, and a further twelve were formed

This Swordfish is in the colour scheme adopted for service in the Indian Ocean.

during the war years. The Swordfish had a distinguished war career, its most notable action being the devastating torpedo attack on the Italian Fleet at Taranto in November 1944.

NOTABLE ACTIONS

Other important Swordfish actions included the Battle of Cape Matapan in March 1941, the crippling of the German battleship *Bismarck* in May, and the gallant action against the *Scharnhorst*, *Gneisenau* and *Prinz Eugen* in the famous 'Channel Dash' of February 1942, when all six Swordfish involved (from No 825 Squadron) were shot down. The Swordfish Mk II, which appeared in 1943, had metal-covered lower wings, enabling it to carry rocket projectiles. The Swordfish Mk III carried ASV radar in a housing between the main landing gear legs. Swordfish production ended on 18

Fairey Swordfish Mk III

Powerplant:	611kW (820hp) Bristol Pegasus XXX radial engine
Performance:	maximum speed 222km/h (138mph); service ceiling 5867m (19250ft); range 879km (546 miles)
Weights:	empty 2132kg (4700lb); maximum take-off 4196kg (9250lb)
Dimensions:	wing span 12.97m (42ft 6in); length 10.87m (35ft 8in); height 3.76m (12ft 4in)
Armament:	two 7.7mm (0.303in) machine guns, plus one 457mm (18in) torpedo or eight 27.2kg (60lb) rocket projectiles

August 1944, by which time 2391 aircraft had been built.

Torpedo-armed Swordfish flying in tight formation on an anti-shipping raid.

UNITED KINGDOM

GLOSTER GLADIATOR

*The Gloster Gladiator was the last of the RAF's
biplane fighters, and although it was obsolescent
at the outbreak of WWII it gave a good
account of itself, especially in the
Mediterranean theatre.*

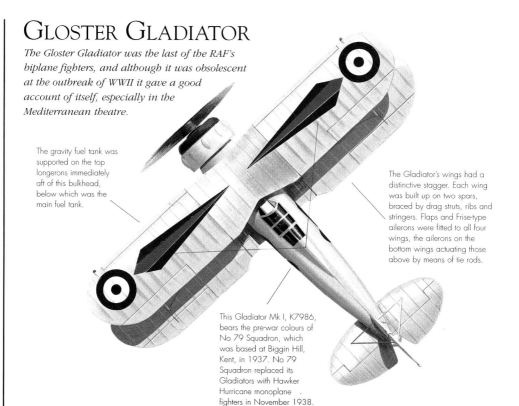

The gravity fuel tank was
supported on the top
longerons immediately
aft of this bulkhead,
below which was the
main fuel tank.

The Gladiator's wings had a
distinctive stagger. Each wing
was built up on two spars,
braced by drag struts, ribs and
stringers. Flaps and Frise-type
ailerons were fitted to all four
wings, the ailerons on the
bottom wings actuating those
above by means of tie rods.

This Gladiator Mk I, K7986,
bears the pre-war colours of
No 79 Squadron, which
was based at Biggin Hill,
Kent, in 1937. No 79
Squadron replaced its
Gladiators with Hawker
Hurricane monoplane
fighters in November 1938.

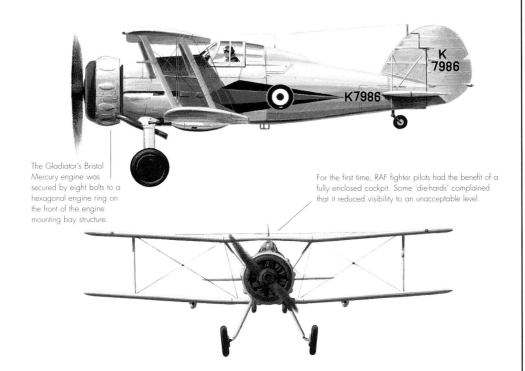

The Gladiator's Bristol Mercury engine was secured by eight bolts to a hexagonal engine ring on the front of the engine mounting bay structure.

For the first time, RAF fighter pilots had the benefit of a fully enclosed cockpit. Some 'die-hards' complained that it reduced visibility to an unacceptable level.

D esigned as a more advanced
successor to the open-cockpit
Gauntlet fighter, the prototype
Gladiator was flown in September 1934 and
evaluated by the Air Ministry in the following
year, the trials resulting in a production order
for 23 machines, followed by further orders
for 128 aircraft. These were powered by

**This Gloster Gladiator has been
lovingly restored to flying condition.**

626kW (840hp) Mercury IXS engines and
were armed with four Vickers machine guns.
First deliveries were made in February 1937,
and the aircraft went on to equip eight
squadrons of Fighter Command.

FOREIGN ORDERS

The Gladiator II was developed to fulfil foreign orders, 147 being produced for this purpose, and 252 were also built for the RAF. The RAF's Gladiators fought in Norway, France, North Africa, the Middle East and the Balkans. Foreign air forces operating the Gladiator were those of Belgium, China, Eire, Greece, Latvia, Lithuania, Norway, Portugal and Sweden.

The naval equivalent, the Sea Gladiator, was an adaptation of the Mk II, and equipped seven Fleet Air Arm squadrons from 1939.

Gloster Gladiator Mk II

Powerplant:	619kW (830hp) Bristol Mercury VIIIA 9-cylinder radial
Performance:	maximum speed 414km/h (257mph); service ceiling 10,210m (33,500ft); maximum range 708km (440 miles)
Weights:	empty 1562kg (3444lb); maximum take-off 2206kg (4864lb)
Dimensions:	wing span 9.83m (32ft 3in); length 8.36m (27ft 5in); height 3.53m (11ft 7in)
Armament:	four 7.7mm (0.303in) machine guns

Three Sea Gladiators, popularly known as Faith, Hope and Charity, famously defended Malta in the summer of 1940.

K6131 was the third production Gladiator Mk I.

GLOSTER METEOR III

Apart from the fact that it was jet-powered, the Gloster Meteor was entirely conventional in design. It served the Royal Air Force – and other air forces – well, until more advanced equipment came along in the 1950s.

The Meteor F.I had a hinged sideways-opening cockpit canopy, but the Mk III was fitted with a one-piece sliding canopy. Pilots coming to the Meteor from piston-engined fighters were astounded by the relative absence of noise in the cockpit.

The Meteor Mks I to IV featured this distinctive tail unit, as did the T.7 trainer version and the photo-reconnaissance PR.10. The last day-fighter version, the F.8, had a much modified and more angular tail, as did the night-fighter variants of the 1950s.

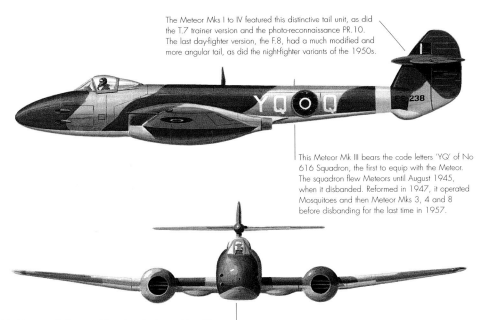

This Meteor Mk III bears the code letters 'YQ' of No 616 Squadron, the first to equip with the Meteor. The squadron flew Meteors until August 1945, when it disbanded. Reformed in 1947, it operated Mosquitoes and then Meteor Mks 3, 4 and 8 before disbanding for the last time in 1957.

The Meteor packed a powerful punch in the shape of four 20mm (0.79in) nose-mounted cannon. In the closing weeks of WWII Meteors carried out ground-attack operations in northwest Europe, but never met the Luftwaffe in action.

UNITED KINGDOM

The Gloster Meteor was the Allies' first operational jet fighter, and was Gloster's answer to Air Ministry specification F.9/40, calling for a single-seat interceptor powered by gas turbine engines. The low thrust output of the engines available at the time dictated a twin-engine configuration, but apart from

Starting the turbines of a Meteor Mk III in Belgium in 1945.

the radical nature of its propulsion the Meteor was entirely conventional in design. The first 20 production aircraft were fitted with 771kg (1700lb) Rolls-Royce Welland engines. Twelve of these were issued to

No 616 Squadron, which began operational patrols against V-1 flying bombs in July 1944.

GROUND ATTACK ROLE

The next variant, the Meteor F.3, was a much better proposition, using the 906kg (2000lb) thrust Rolls-Royce Derwent I engine; but deliveries to No 616 Squadron did not begin until December 1944. The Mk III version, eventually equipped 15 squadrons of RAF Fighter Command in the immediate post-war years, and was operational in a ground-attack role in the closing weeks of the war. It was followed into service by the Meteor

Gloster Meteor F. Mk III

Powerplant:	two 906kg (2000lb) thrust Rolls-Royce Derwent 1 turbojets
Performance:	Maximum speed 675km/h (415mph) at 3050m (10,000ft); service ceiling 13,106m (43,000ft); range 1580km (982 miles)
Weights:	empty 4771kg (10,520lb); maximum take-off 6314kg (13,920lb)
Dimensions:	wing span 13.10m (43ft); length 12.50m (41ft); height 3.96m (13ft)
Armament:	four 20mm (0.79in) cannon

F.Mk.4. Powered by two Rolls-Royce Derwent 5s, the F. Mk IV first flew in April 1945 and subsequently, in November, set a new world air speed record of 975km/h (606mph).

Meteor III EE457 was the first to feature elongated engine nacelles.

HANDLEY PAGE HALIFAX

*Though less famous than the Lancaster and capable
of slightly lesser performance, the Halifax served RAF
Bomber Command well in operations
over Germany.*

The Halifax Mk III was fitted with
Bristol Hercules engines, but the
earlier marks, with Rolls-Royce
Merlins, had a longer range, and
these were retained by the special
duties squadrons for infiltrating
agents into enemy territory.

Late model Halifaxes
were equipped with two
types of rear turret: either
the Type D with twin
12.7mm (0.50in)
machine guns or the
Type E with four 7.62mm
(0.30in) guns.

The dorsal turret was a Boulton Paul A Mk III mid-upper turret, armed with four 7.62mm (0.30in) guns with 1160 rounds each. The teardrop fairing on top of the fuselage between cockpit and dorsal turret housed the direction finder aerial.

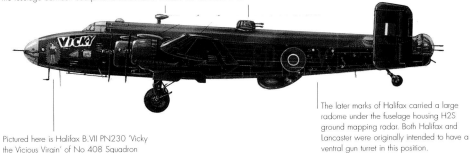

The later marks of Halifax carried a large radome under the fuselage housing H2S ground mapping radar. Both Halifax and Lancaster were originally intended to have a ventral gun turret in this position.

Pictured here is Halifax B.VII PN230 'Vicky the Vicious Virgin' of No 408 Squadron RCAF, RAF Linton-on-Ouse, Yorkshire, 1945.

UNITED KINGDOM

The prototype HP.57 Halifax flew for the first time on 25 October 1939, followed by a second aircraft in August 1939. Early production aircraft became known as the Halifax Mk I Series I, which was followed by the Mk I Series II with a higher gross weight and the Series III, with increased fuel tankage. The first major

A fine wartime colour photograph of a Halifax Mk I of No 35 Squadron.

modification appeared in the Mk II Series I, which had a two-gun dorsal turret and uprated 1037kW (1390hp) XX engines. The Mk II Series I (Special) had a fairing in place of the nose turret, and the engine exhaust muffs were omitted, while the Mk II Series IA was the first variant to introduce the drag-reducing moulded Perspex nose that was a feature of all subsequent Halifaxes, a four-gun dorsal turret, and Merlin 22 engines. The Mk II Series IA also had large, rectangular vertical tail surfaces, as serious control difficulties had been experienced with the original tail configuration.

HERCULES ENGINES

In 1943 the Merlin engines were replaced by four 1204kW (1615hp) Bristol Hercules XVI radial engines in the Halifax Mk III, which remained in the front line up to the end of the war. The next operational variants were the Mks VI and VII, the former powered by the 1249kW (1675hp) Hercules 100 and the latter using the MK III's Hercules XVI. These were the ultimate bomber versions, and were produced in relatively small numbers. The Halifax Mks VIII and IX were transport versions. Various marks of Halifax also

Handley Page Halifax Mk III

Powerplant:	four 1204kW (1615hp) Bristol Hercules VI or XVI 14-cylinder two-row radial engines
Performance:	maximum speed 454km/h (282mph) at 4115m (13,500ft); service ceiling 7315m (24,000ft); range 3194km (1985 miles)
Weights:	empty 17690kg (39,000lb); maximum take-off 30,845kg (68,000lb)
Dimensions:	wing span 30.07m (98ft 8in); length 21.82m (71ft 7in); height 6.32m (20ft 9in)
Armament:	five 7.62mm (0.30in) machine guns, plus an internal bomb load of 6577kg (14,500lb)

served with some squadrons of RAF Coastal Command. The total Halifax production figure was 6176 aircraft.

HAWKER HURRICANE MK IIC

Although overshadowed in the Battle of Britain by the more glamorous Spitfire, the Hawker Hurricane continued to prove its worth as a fighter-bomber in other theatres of war.

UNITED KINGDOM

This Hurricane Mk IIc, based in Egypt with No 94 Squadron in 1942, carries the normal camouflage for RAF fighters in that theatre – dark earth, middle stone and azure blue. No 94 Squadron served in the Middle East and Mediterranean throughout the war, disbanding in Greece in April 1945.

This Hurricane, HL851, was one of three Hurricane Mk IIs donated by Lady Rachel MacRobert of Douneside and Cromar in memory of her three sons who had all been killed flying with the RAF in the early part of the war.

198

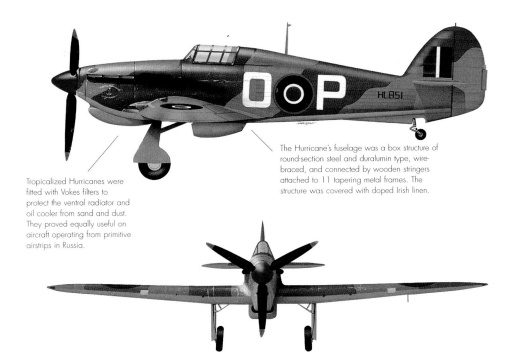

Tropicalized Hurricanes were fitted with Vokes filters to protect the ventral radiator and oil cooler from sand and dust. They proved equally useful on aircraft operating from primitive airstrips in Russia.

The Hurricane's fuselage was a box structure of round-section steel and duralumin type, wire-braced, and connected by wooden stringers attached to 11 tapering metal frames. The structure was covered with doped Irish linen.

UNITED KINGDOM

Designed by Sydney Camm to meet Air Ministry Specification F.36/34, the prototype Hurricane flew on 6 November 1935, powered by a Merlin 'C' engine of 738kW (990hp), and production Hurricane Is were delivered to No 111 Squadron in November. The Mk II Hurricane was fitted with a Merlin XX engine. Early Mk

Mk II Hurricanes in the Western Desert preparing for a sortie.

IIs, which retained the eight-gun armament, were designated Mk IIAs; with 12 machine guns the designation became Mk IIB, while the Mk IIC had a wing armament of four 20mm (0.79in) Hispano cannon.

ANTI-TANK VERSION

The Mk IID was a special anti-tank version, armed with two underwing 40mm (1.57in) Vickers 'S' guns and two 7.62mm (0.30in) Brownings in the wings. Both IIBs and IICs were fitted with cameras and used for reconnaissance as the Mks PR.IIB and PR.IIC. As Hurricanes were progressively withdrawn from first-line RAF squadrons they were converted for naval use as Sea Hurricanes Mks IB, IIC and XIIA.

Overall Hurricane production in the UK was 13,080; another 1451 Mks X, XI, XII and XIIA, fitted with various armament combinations and Packard-built Rolls-Royce

Hawker Hurricane Mk IIC

Powerplant:	1089kW (1460hp) Rolls-Royce Merlin XX 12-cylinder V-type
Performance:	maximum speed 518km/h (322mph) at 5425m (17,800ft); service ceiling 9785m (32,100ft); range: 1448km (900 miles)
Weights:	empty 2566kg (5658lb); maximum take-off 3674kg (8100lb)
Dimensions:	wing span 12.19m (40ft); length 9.81m (32ft 2.25in); height 3.98m (13ft 1in)
Armament:	two 20mm (0.79in) Hispano cannon; up to 454kg (1000lb) of bombs on underwing racks

Merlins, were produced by the Canadian Car and Foundry Co.

Hurricane IIs of No 94 Squadron over the Middle East.

HAWKER TEMPEST MK V

The Hawker Tempest was the most powerful RAF fighter of World War II, and performed admirably in the air superiority role in the final months of the conflict.

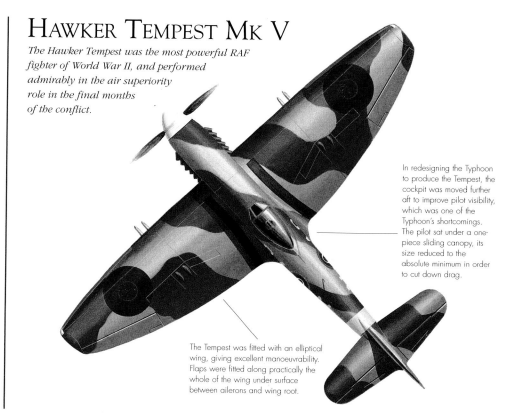

In redesigning the Typhoon to produce the Tempest, the cockpit was moved further aft to improve pilot visibility, which was one of the Typhoon's shortcomings. The pilot sat under a one-piece sliding canopy, its size reduced to the absolute minimum in order to cut down drag.

The Tempest was fitted with an elliptical wing, giving excellent manoeuvrability. Flaps were fitted along practically the whole of the wing under surface between ailerons and wing root.

The tail unit was completely redesigned, the area of the tail fin being doubled to ensure maximum stability at high speeds.

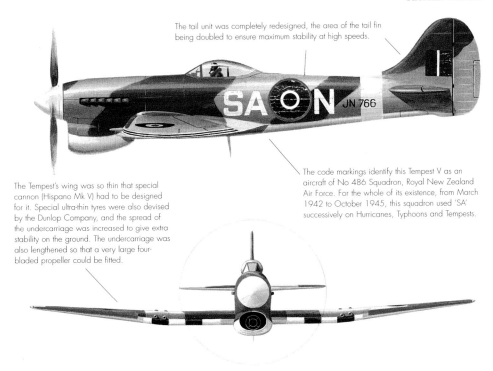

The code markings identify this Tempest V as an aircraft of No 486 Squadron, Royal New Zealand Air Force. For the whole of its existence, from March 1942 to October 1945, this squadron used 'SA' successively on Hurricanes, Typhoons and Tempests.

The Tempest's wing was so thin that special cannon (Hispano Mk V) had to be designed for it. Special ultra-thin tyres were also devised by the Dunlop Company, and the spread of the undercarriage was increased to give extra stability on the ground. The undercarriage was also lengthened so that a very large four-bladed propeller could be fitted.

UNITED KINGDOM

A superb airborne study of Tempest V EJ743 over southern England.

Developed to Specification F.10/41, the Hawker Tempest V was in effect a radical redesign of the Typhoon. The prototype Tempest I flew on 2 September 1942 and an initial contract called for 400 Tempest Is, powered by the Napier Sabre IV engine, but this was cancelled and the contract amended in favour of the Centaurus-powered Tempest Mk II. Delays in the production of this engine, however, and the cancellation of the projected Tempest Mks III and IV, meant that the first variant to enter production was the Tempest Mk V, powered by the Napier Sabre II.

In April 1944 the Tempest was the fastest and most powerful fighter in the world, and in the summer of 1944 it was thrown into battle against the V-1 flying bombs that were now being launched against London. Between them, the Tempest squadrons claimed the destruction of nearly 600 V-1s. The Tempest squadrons subsequently moved to the Continent with 2nd TAF and became a potent addition to the Allies' striking power during the closing months of the war. Eleven squadrons were eventually armed with the Tempest Mk V and five with the Mk VI, which

Hawker Tempest Mk V

Powerplant:	1685kW (2260hp) Napier Sabre IIA, IIB or IIC 24-cylinder H-type engine
Performance:	maximum speed 700km/h (435mph); service ceiling 10,975m (36,000ft); range 2092km (1300 miles)
Weights:	empty 4854kg (10,700lb); maximum take-off 6187kg (13,640lb)
Dimensions:	wing span 12.50m (41ft); length 10.26m (33ft 8in); height 4.90m (16ft 1in)
Armament:	four 20mm (0.79in) cannon; bombs or rockets up to 907kg (2000lb)

had a 2013kW (2700hp) Sabre VA engine. Total Tempest V production was 805 aircraft.

The Tempest V of Wng Cdr R. Beamont, who pioneered the type into service.

HAWKER TYPHOON MK IB

*Intended as an all-altitude interceptor, the
Hawker Typhoon proved inadequate in this
role except at low level, but it went on to
make its mark as the most potent
Allied fighter-bomber.*

The Typhoon's wing
was built around an
immensely strong two-
spar structure. Mounted
in the port wing just
outboard of the landing
light was a gun camera
to record rocket and
cannon strikes.

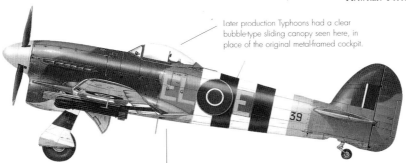

Later production Typhoons had a clear bubble-type sliding canopy seen here, in place of the original metal-framed cockpit.

The Typhoon's underwing hardpoints could accommodate eight 27kg (60lb) rockets, as illustrated, or two bombs of up to 453kg (1000lb) in weight. The four 20mm (0.79in) Hispano cannon were armed with 120 rounds per gun.

This Typhoon IB carries the code letters of No 181 Squadron. In the early part of 1944 the squadron's Typhoons carried out many attacks on V-1 flying bomb sites before moving to France after D-Day in support of the Allied armies.

A large air intake under the chin admitted all air for engine and oil cooling. In the centre was a ram air inlet for the supercharger, surrounded by an annular radiator for oil cooling. The engine radiator was outside this.

UNITED KINGDOM

A cantilever low-wing monoplane of basically all-metal stressed-skin construction with a retractable tailwheel, the Hawker Typhoon was designed to combat heavily armed and armoured escort fighters like the Messerschmitt Bf 110. The first of two prototypes, powered by a 1566kW (2100hp)

A rocket-armed Hawker Typhoon IB in Normandy, 1944.

Napier Sabre H-type inline engine, flew for the first time on 24 February 1940. However, the aircraft suffered from constant teething troubles, and the first Typhoon squadron (No 56) did not become operational until May

1942, being assigned to air defence operations against low-level intruders.

POTENT FIGHTER-BOMBER

The Typhoon MK 1A, which was armed with 12 7.7mm (0.303in) machine guns, soon gave way to the Mk 1B, whose four 20mm (0.79in) cannon proved effective in the ground-attack role and which was powered by the more reliable 1625kW (2180hp) Sabre IIA engine. By the end of 1943 the Typhoon was heading for its place in history as the most potent Allied fighter-bomber. In all, 3330 Typhoons were built, all by Gloster

Hawker Typhoon Mk IB

Typical powerplant:	1625kW (2180hp) Napier Sabre IIA 24-cylinder in-line
Performance:	maximum speed 663km/h (412mph); service ceiling 10,730m (35,200ft); range 1577km (980 miles) with external tanks
Weights:	empty 3992kg (8800lb); maximum take-off 6010kg (13,250lb)
Dimensions:	wing span 12.67m (41ft 7in); length 9.73m (31ft 11in); height 4.67m (15ft 4in)
Armament:	four 20mm (0.79in) fixed forward-firing cannon in wing, plus eight 27kg (60lb) rockets

except for the two prototypes, five Mk 1As and ten Mk 1Bs.

Typhoon 1B HF-L of No 183 Squadron, pictured in 1943.

SHORT STIRLING

Throughout its operational life, the Short Stirling suffered from an Air Ministry instruction which dictated that its wing span should be reduced so that the aircraft would fit inside existing hangars. Its altitude performance suffered accordingly.

Though stable in flight and surprisingly manoeuvrable, thanks to its high wing loading, the Stirling had a poor operational ceiling when loaded, often being hard pushed to climb above 3660m (12,000ft). This was due to the aircraft's 30.48m (100ft) span wing, a reduced size made necessary by the size of pre-war RAF hangars.

To shorten take-offs and landings the Stirling was fitted with a very tall undercarriage. This gave the aircraft a pronounced nose-up attitude when on the ground, and a sufficient angle of incidence to provide adequate lift during the take-off run, but made ground handling tricky.

This Stirling carries the code letters of No 7 Squadron, the first to equip with the type in August 1940. The squadron was than at RAF Leeming, in Yorkshire, but in October 1940 it moved to Oakington, near Cambridge, and remained there for the rest of the war, by which time it was using Lancasters.

The Stirling suffered from troublesome undercarriage retraction motors, which proved inadequate for the task. The main wheels were the largest fitted to an operational aircraft during World War II.

UNITED KINGDOM

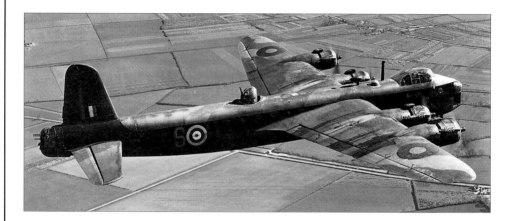

The first of the RAF's trio of four-engined heavy bombers, the other two being the Halifax and Lancaster, the Short Stirling was designed to a 1936 specification and was first flown as a half-scale prototype in 1938. The full-scale prototype flew in May 1939 and was damaged beyond repair on its first flight

The Stirling suffered from a poor ceiling, due to a reduction in its wing span.

when its undercarriage collapsed. Production deliveries of the Stirling Mk I were made to No 7 Squadron in August 1940, the squadron flying its first operational sortie, an attack on an oil storage depot at

Rotterdam, on 10/11 February 1941. The main bomber variant was the Stirling Mk III, which had Hercules XVI engines and a two-gun dorsal turret.

TRANSPORT AND GLIDER TUG

Stirlings flew their last bombing mission in September 1944, having equipped 15 squadrons of RAF Bomber Command. By this time the aircraft had found a new role as a transport and glider tug (Stirling Mk IV). The

Short Stirling Mk I

Powerplant:	four 1230kW (1650hp) Bristol Hercules XVI 14-cylinder radials
Performance:	maximum speed 434km/h (270mph) at 4420m (14,500ft); service ceiling 5180m (17,000ft); range 3235km (2010 miles)
Weights:	empty 21,274kg (46,900lb); maximum take-off 31,752kg (70,000lb)
Dimensions:	wing span 30.20m (99ft 1in); length 26.59m (87ft 3in); height 6.93m (22ft 9in)
Armament:	six 7.7mm (0.303in) machine guns plus internal bomb load of 6350kg (14,000lb)

last variant was the unarmed Mk V transport, which entered service in January 1945.

Ground crew loading mines on to a Stirling at RAF Lakenheath.

UNITED KINGDOM

SHORT SUNDERLAND MK III

Dubbed the 'Flying Porcupine' because of its heavy defensive armament, the Short Sunderland flying boat proved to be a vital weapon in the Battle of the Atlantic, and was to become one of the RAF's longest-serving operational aircraft.

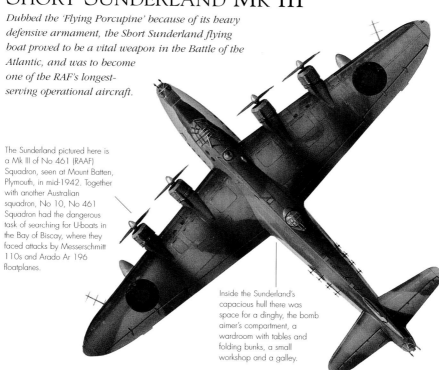

The Sunderland pictured here is a Mk III of No 461 (RAAF) Squadron, seen at Mount Batten, Plymouth, in mid-1942. Together with another Australian squadron, No 10, No 461 Squadron had the dangerous task of searching for U-boats in the Bay of Biscay, where they faced attacks by Messerschmitt 110s and Arado Ar 196 floatplanes.

Inside the Sunderland's capacious hull there was space for a dinghy, the bomb aimer's compartment, a wardroom with tables and folding bunks, a small workshop and a galley.

The ASV Mk III radar carried by the Sunderland Mk III was an adaptation of Bomber Command's H2S navigational radar system. It was later replaced by the ASV Mk VIc 9-centimetre radar, the search antenna for which was housed in split scanners under the wingtips.

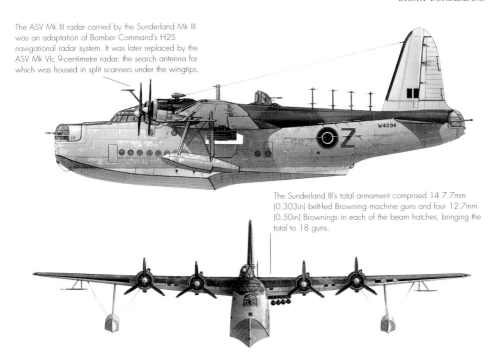

The Sunderland III's total armament comprised 14 7.7mm (0.303in) belt-fed Browning machine guns and four 12.7mm (0.50in) Brownings in each of the beam hatches, bringing the total to 18 guns.

The design of the Sunderland was based on that of the stately Short C Class 'Empire' flying boats operated by Imperial Airways in the 1930s. The prototype first flew on 16 October 1937, and the first production Sunderland Mk Is were delivered to No 230 Squadron in Singapore early in June 1938. By the outbreak of World

The Sunderland made an impressive sight when taking off and alighting.

War II in September 1939 three more squadrons were equipped with the type. The Sunderland Mk I, of which 90 were built, was followed by 55 Mk IIs; these were fitted with Pegasus XVIII engines with two-stage supercharges, a twin-gun dorsal turret, an improved rear turret and ASV Mk II radar. The major production version was the Mk III, with a modified hull; 456 were built by Shorts and Blackburn Aircraft.

COMMERCIAL USE

The Sunderland IV was a larger and heavier development with 1267kW (1700hp) Bristol Hercules engines; only ten aircraft were built. They were later converted for commercial use as the Short Solent. The last operational Sunderland was the Mk V, which remained in first-line service with No 205 Squadron at Changi, Singapore, until 1959.

Short Sunderland Mk III

Powerplant:	four 895kW (1200hp) Pratt & Whitney R-1830-90 Twin Wasp 14-cylinder radial engines
Performance:	maximum speed 349km/h (217mph) at 1525m (5000ft); service ceiling 5445m (17,900ft); range 4796km (2980 miles)
Weights:	empty 16,738kg (36,900lb); maximum take-off 27,216kg (60,000lb)
Dimensions:	wing span 34.36m (112ft 9.5in); length 26.00m (85ft 3.5in); height 10.52m (34ft 6in)
Armament:	fourteen 7.7mm (0.303in) machine guns, and four 12.7mm (0.50in) machine guns, plus up to 2250kg (4960lb) of bombs, mines or depth charges

Although effective as a patrol aircraft, the Sunderland lacked range.

UNITED KINGDOM

UNITED KINGDOM

SUPERMARINE SEAFIRE

With its narrow-track undercarriage and long nose, the Supermarine Seafire was far from ideal for aircraft carrier operations, but despite many accidents it served the Royal Navy well in all theatres of war.

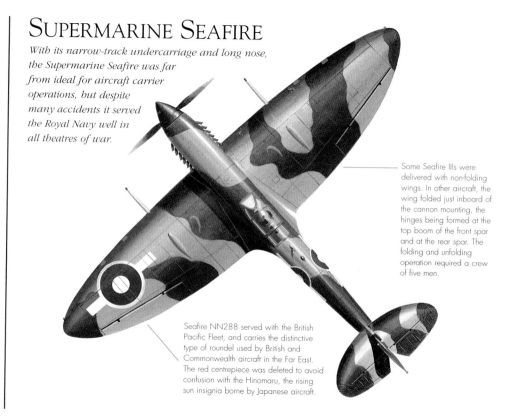

Some Seafire IIIs were delivered with non-folding wings. In other aircraft, the wing folded just inboard of the cannon mounting, the hinges being formed at the top boom of the front spar and at the rear spar. The folding and unfolding operation required a crew of five men.

Seafire NN288 served with the British Pacific Fleet, and carries the distinctive type of roundel used by British and Commonwealth aircraft in the Far East. The red centrepiece was deleted to avoid confusion with the Hinomaru, the rising sun insignia borne by Japanese aircraft.

All Seafire IIIs could carry two 113kg (250lb) bombs under the wings or a single 227kg (500lb) bomb under the fuselage. Provision was also made for the fitting of a 30-gallon drop tank in place of the single bomb. The Seafire could be fitted with Rocket-Assisted Take-Off Gear (RATOG).

This Seafire, NN288, was one of a batch of 200 aircraft ordered from Westland Aircraft on 5 January 1943 and delivered from April 1944 as LF Mk IIIs with Merlin 55m engines.

UNITED KINGDOM

219

Between the two world wars, the Royal Navy's carrier-borne aircraft evolved at a much slower pace than their land-based counterparts. With the outbreak of WWII the RN found a partial solution to the problem by adapting land-based aircraft like the Hawker Hurricane for carrier operations, and in late 1941 it was

A Supermarine Seafire fitted with rocket-assisted take-off equipment.

decided to adapt the Spitfire in similar fashion under the name of Seafire. The main variants were the Seafire Mk IB (166 conversions from Spitfire VB airframes); Mk IIC (372 intended for low- and medium-altitude air combat and air reconnaissance); 30 Mk III (Hybrid) aircraft with fixed wings, followed by 1220 examples of the definitive Seafire Mk III with folding wings; and the Seafire Mks XV, XVII, 45, 46 and 47, these being Griffon-engined variants.

MEDITERRANEAN ACTION

The Seafire saw much action in the Mediterranean in the summer of 1943 and in the Pacific in 1945. The Seafire 47, operating from HMS *Triumph*, took part in air strikes against terrorists in Malaya and against North Korean forces in the early weeks of the Korean War. The Seafire

Supermarine Seafire Mk III

Powerplant:	1193kW (1600hp) Rolls-Royce Merlin 55m 12-cylinder V-type
Performance:	maximum speed 560km/h (348mph) at 3050m (10,000ft); service ceiling 7315m (24,000ft); range 890km (553 miles)
Weights:	empty 2814kg (6204lb); maximum take-off 3465kg (7640lb)
Dimensions:	wing span 11.23m (36ft 10in); length 9.21m (30ft 2.5in); height 3.42m (11ft 2.5in)
Armament:	two 20mm cannon and four 7.7mm (0.303in) machine guns; external bomb or rocket load of 227kg (500lb)

remained in service with RN Reserve Air Squadrons until 1954.

The Seafire 47, in service at the start of the Korean War, was the last of the line.

SUPERMARINE SPITFIRE FR.MK XIVE

The famous Supermarine Spitfire, which began its operational career as an interceptor fighter, went on to perform many and varied tasks, one of which was low-level tactical reconnaissance – a role to which it was well suited.

Most Mk XIVEs had 'clipped' wings to improve agility at low altitude, and had a one-piece 'teardrop' cockpit canopy to enhance all-round visibility. All Mk XIVs were equipped with broad chord tails to counteract the torque of the Griffon engine.

For the tactical reconnaissance role the FR.Mk XIV carried a single oblique camera mounted in a bay behind the cockpit and arranged to point to port or starboard, as required.

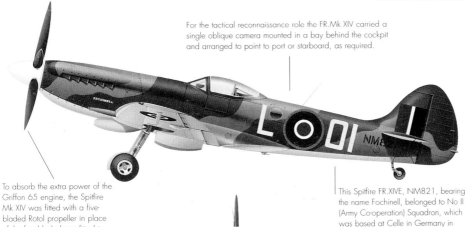

To absorb the extra power of the Griffon 65 engine, the Spitfire Mk XIV was fitted with a five-bladed Rotol propeller in place of the four-bladed one fitted to the Mk XII.

This Spitfire FR.XIVE, NM821, bearing the name Fochinell, belonged to No II (Army Co-operation) Squadron, which was based at Celle in Germany in September 1945 as part of the British Air Forces of Occupation. The squadron used various marks of Spitfire until 1951.

As was the case with the Merlin engine, the performance of the Griffon engine at altitude was enhanced by the introduction of two-stage supercharging.

The Spitfire FR.Mk XIVE was one of the later Griffon-engined variants of Reginald Mitchell's famous design, the first of which, the Mk XII, was developed specifically to counter the low-level attacks by Focke-Wulf 190s. Only 100 MK XII Spitfires were built, but they were followed by the more numerous Mk XIV.

Spitfire Mk XIV bearing the markings of No 322 (Dutch) Squadron.

The latter, based on a Mk VIII airframe strengthened to cope with the stresses and vibrations of a more powerful engine than the Merlin, was the first Griffon-engined Spitfire variant to go into large-scale production, and the first were issued to No 322 (Netherlands) and No 610 Squadrons in March and April 1944.

GROUND-ATTACK VERSION

The Spitfire XVI, which entered service in 1944, was a ground-attack version similar to the Mk IX, but with a Packard-built Merlin 266 engine. The Spitfire XVIII was a fighter-reconnaissance variant, just beginning to enter service at the end of WWII, as was the PR Mk XIX. The last variants of the Spitfire, produced until 1947, were the Mks 21, 22 and 24. They bore very little resemblance to the prototype Mk I of a decade earlier. Total

Supermarine Spitfire FR.Mk XIVE

Powerplant:	1529kW (2050hp) Rolls-Royce Griffon 65 12-cylinder Vee-type engine
Performance:	721km/h (448mph) at 7468m (24,500ft); service ceiling 13,565m (44,500ft); range 756km (470 miles)
Weights:	empty 2994kg (6600lb); maximum take-off 3856kg (8500lb)
Dimensions:	wing span 11.23m (36ft 10in); length 9.11m (29ft 11in); height 3.48m (11ft 5in)
Armament:	two 20mm (0.79in) cannon and two 12.7mm (0.50in) machine guns

production of the Spitfire was 20,351, plus 2334 of the naval version, the Seafire.

A Spitfire XIV; note the powerful Griffon engine, and the five-bladed propeller.

UNITED KINGDOM

BELL P-63 KINGCOBRA

Seen here is one of the many P-63s supplied to the Soviet Union under Lend-Lease arrangements. The Russians found the P-63 to be an excellent ground-attack aircraft.

The P-63 was armed with a 37mm (1.46in) M4 cannon firing through the propeller boss; two of the four 12.7mm (0.50in) machine guns were mounted in the upper forward fuselage.

The air scoop on the upper fuselage was situated far enough back so that the cockpit canopy had plenty of clearance when it slid open to the rear.

The P-63 was fitted with a laminar-flow wing which was aerodynamically very clean and reduced drag.

The Allison engine was situated in the middle fuselage bay, driving a long crankshaft that passed between the pilot's legs.

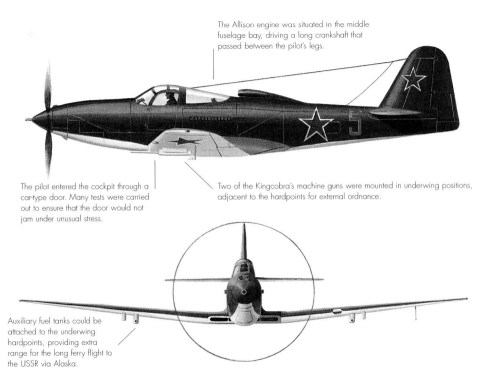

The pilot entered the cockpit through a car-type door. Many tests were carried out to ensure that the door would not jam under unusual stress.

Two of the Kingcobra's machine guns were mounted in underwing positions, adjacent to the hardpoints for external ordnance.

Auxiliary fuel tanks could be attached to the underwing hardpoints, providing extra range for the long ferry flight to the USSR via Alaska.

UNITED STATES

The Bell P-63 Kingcobra design had its origin in a modified Airacobra, the XP-39E, which was an attempt to update the inadequate P-39 series of aircraft by means of some fairly drastic modifications. The basic P-39 fuselage was left intact, but the three experimental XP-39Es were fitted with a new laminar-flow

The French Air Force took delivery of some 300 P-63C Kingcobras at the end of the war.

wing with square tips, and each had a redesigned tail unit. Two XP-63 prototypes were built, the first of which flew on 7 December 1942.

GUNNERY TARGETS

The aircraft was intended to succeed the P-39 in the fighter and fighter-bomber roles, but only 332 were in fact delivered to the USAAF and were used as ground-based gunnery targets with the designations RP-63A, RP-63C and RP-63G. No Airacobra ever saw combat with the USAAF. Of the 1725 P-63A and 1227 P-63C Kingcobras built, 2421 were supplied to the USSR under Lend-Lease, proving to be excellent ground-attack aircraft, and 300 were allocated to the Free French Air Force. Some of these were

Bell P-63A Kingcobra

Powerplant:	988kW (1325hp) Allison V-1710-95 V-type
Performance:	max speed 657km/h (408mph) at 7452m (24,450ft); service ceiling 13,105m (43,000ft); range: 724km (450 miles)
Weights:	empty 2892kg (6375lb); maximum take-off 4763kg (10,500lb)
Dimensions:	wing span 11.68m (38ft 4in) length 9.96m (32ft 8in); height: 3.84m (12ft 7in)
Armament:	one 37mm (1.46in) gun and four 12.7mm (0.50in) guns; provision for three 227kg (500lb) bombs

deployed to French Indo-China, where they were ill-suited to the tropical conditions.

USAAF Kingcobras were used as fighter trainers, and did not see combat.

BOEING B-17G FLYING FORTRESS

The aircraft pictured here is a Fortress B.Mk III (B-17G) of No 214 (Special Duties) Squadron, which was based at Oulton, Norfolk in 1944 and which formed part of No 100 (Bomber Support) Group RAF.

The aerial between the tail guns was for a tail warning receiver code-named Monica. This was designed to detect enemy night fighter radars.

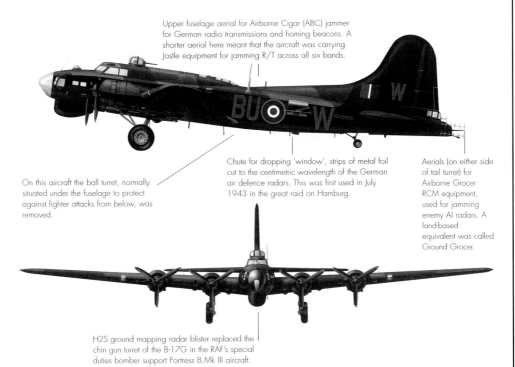

Upper fuselage aerial for Airborne Cigar (ABC) jammer for German radio transmissions and homing beacons. A shorter aerial here meant that the aircraft was carrying Jostle equipment for jamming R/T across all six bands.

Chute for dropping 'window', strips of metal foil cut to the centimetric wavelength of the German air defence radars. This was first used in July 1943 in the great raid on Hamburg.

On this aircraft the ball turret, normally situated under the fuselage to protect against fighter attacks from below, was removed.

Aerials (on either side of tail turret) for Airborne Grocer RCM equipment, used for jamming enemy AI radars. A land-based equivalent was called Ground Grocer.

H2S ground mapping radar blister replaced the chin gun turret of the B-17G in the RAF's special duties bomber support Fortress B.Mk III aircraft.

UNITED STATES

To fulfil its vital electronic counter-measures and a bomber support role, the Royal Air Force obtained 14 B-17F Flying Fortresses for operations with No 100 Group; these were later supplemented by some B-17Gs. Modifications included the replacement of the B-17G's chin turret by an H2S blister, the provision of mufflers to

The B-17 made a huge contribution to the Allied strategic bombing offensive.

screen exhaust flames and the fitting of jamming devices in the bomb bay. A variety of radio countermeasures (RCM) equipment was carried, including devices code-named Jostle and Piperack. The first, a high-powered communications jammer, emitted a high-pitched wail and could effectively jam any frequency used by the German fighter controllers. The second, developed from an American RCM kit called Dina, covered the 90-110 mc/s frequency used by the German AI radars. The aircraft began operations with No 214 Squadron in June 1944. In addition, B-17s of the 803rd Squadron, United States Strategic Air Forces were also equipped for the jamming role, and this unit was placed under the operational control of No 100 Group. A third squadron, No 223, which was equipped with Liberators and Fortresses and which began operations in September 1944, was also equipped with these devices.

Boeing B-17G Flying Fortress

Powerplant:	four 895kW (1200hp) Wright Cyclone R-1820-97 radial engines
Performance:	max speed 486km/h (302mph) at 7620m (25,000ft); service ceiling 10,850m (35,600ft); range 3220km (2000 miles) with 2722kg (6000lb) bomb load
Weights:	empty 16,381kg (36,113lb); maximum take-off 32,660kg (72,000lb)
Dimensions:	wing span 31.62m (103ft 9in); length 22.78m (74ft 9in); height 5.82m (19ft 1in)
Armament:	twelve 12.7mm (0.50in) machine guns plus bomb load of 7983kg (17,600lb)

The B-17G was fitted with a chin turret to counter head-on attacks.

UNITED STATES

BOEING B-29 SUPERFORTRESS

Developed as a result of prolonged design studies to be a 'super bomber' capable of attacking targets at extreme ranges, the Superfortress was the heaviest combat aircraft of WWII.

The B-29 was the first aircraft in quantity production with a pressurized fuselage, enhancing crew comfort during long flights.

The B-29 was a third again as large as the B-17. The greatest difference was in the long, narrow wing into which the Wright Cyclone engines were faired.

The rear gunner sat in a pressurized turret with armoured windscreens, controlling a battery of two 12.7mm (0.50in) machine guns and one 20mm (0.79in) cannon. There was no access to the turret in flight.

The Superfortress's heavy armament included a four-gun turret over the nose. This, together with a two-gun turret underneath, provided effective defence against frontal attack.

All gun turrets were remotely controlled, reducing their size and therefore cutting down drag. Everything possible was done to ensure a smooth airflow.

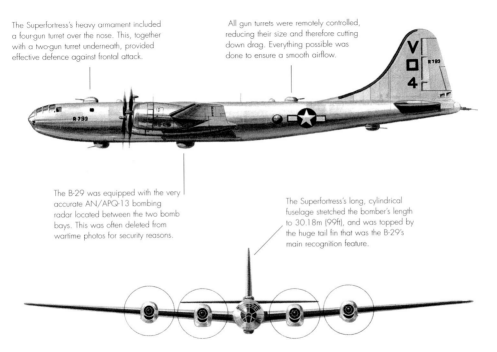

The B-29 was equipped with the very accurate AN/APQ-13 bombing radar located between the two bomb bays. This was often deleted from wartime photos for security reasons.

The Superfortress's long, cylindrical fuselage stretched the bomber's length to 30.18m (99ft), and was topped by the huge tail fin that was the B-29's main recognition feature.

UNITED STATES

amous as the aircraft that dropped the atomic bombs in Hiroshima and Nagasaki, the Boeing B-29 was designed to meet a 1937 requirement for a very long range bomber, Japan's aggressive actions in the Far East having caused a dramatic rise in international tension. By the time the first XB-29 flew on 21 September

Several B-29s were converted to tankers. This KB-29 is refuelling two RAF Meteor Mk 8 jet fighters.

1942 orders for 1500 aircraft had already been placed, the B29 programme having been given maximum priority following the Japanese attack on Pearl Harbor. The first YB-

29 evaluation aircraft were delivered to the 58th Bombardment Wing in July 1943, B-29-BW production aircraft following three months later. The other main versions of the B-29 that made their appearance during the war were the B-29A-BN with a four-gun forward upper turret and increased wing span, and the B-29B-BA with a reduced gun armament and increased bomb load.

OPERATIONAL BASES

A reconnaissance version was designated F-13A (later RB-29). The B-29 incorporated many technical innovations, including remotely controlled gun turrets, periscopically sighted by gunners seated within the fuselage. Operations against Japan from bases in China began in June 1944, operational bases later being established in the Marianas. All B-29 bombardment wings in the Pacific came under the control of XXI Bomber Command. The basic B-29 design underwent several specialist modifications.

B-29 Superfortress

Powerplant:	four 1640kW (2200hp) Wright R-3350-57 radial engines
Performance:	max speed 576km/h (358mph) at 7620m (25,000ft); service ceiling 9695m (31,800ft); range: 6598km (4100 miles)
Weights:	empty 32,369kg (71,360lb); maximum take-off 64,003kg (141,100lb)
Dimensions:	wing span: 43.36m (142ft 3in); length 30.18m (99ft); height: 9.01m (29ft 7in)
Armament:	twelve 12.7mm (0.50in) and one 20mm (0.79in) machine guns, plus bomb load of up to 9072kg (20,000lb)

These included the SB-29 search and rescue aircraft, TB-29 trainer, WB-29 weather reconnaissance aircraft and KB-29 tanker.

UNITED STATES

CONSOLIDATED B-24J LIBERATOR

The B-24 Liberator was notable for its long range, which made it ideal for operations in the Pacific and for attacks on targets in the Balkans from bases in North Africa.

The B-24J Liberator was fitted with a Motor Products nose turret, new-type autopilot and bombsight. The bombardier's position was just below the gun turret, with the navigator just behind it.

The main recognition feature of the B-24, apart from its distinctive twin tail fins, was the long, high aspect ratio wing.

The rear gunner sat in a Consolidated or Motor Products turret manning two 12.7mm (0.50in) machine guns. These were fed from a magazine situated amidships.

The dorsal turret behind the flight deck was manned by the radio operator, to defend the aircraft against attack from above.

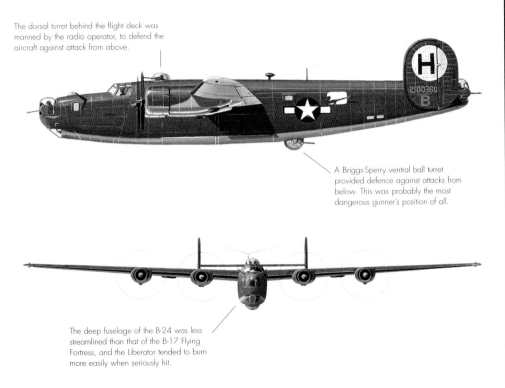

A Briggs-Sperry ventral ball turret provided defence against attacks from below. This was probably the most dangerous gunner's position of all.

The deep fuselage of the B-24 was less streamlined than that of the B-17 Flying Fortress, and the Liberator tended to burn more easily when seriously hit.

UNITED STATES

239

UNITED STATES

The Consolidated B-24 Liberator was built in larger numbers than any other US warplane of World War II, 18,431 being produced in total, and was delivered in greater quantities than any other bomber in aviation history. The XB-24 prototype flew for the first time on 29 December 1939 and was followed by seven

A colourful B-24 Liberator of the 448th Bombardment Group.

YB-24 service evaluation aircraft. The first major production models were the B-24D (2738 aircraft), the generally similar B-24E (791 aircraft) and B-24G (430 aircraft) with a power-operated nose turret.

RAF SERVICE

Further developments of the Liberator were the B-24H, 738 of which were built by Consolidated and 2362 of which were produced by Douglas and Ford; the B-24J, an improved B-24H with an autopilot and other operational upgrades, including a more effective bombsight (6678 aircraft); the B-24L with two manually operated tail guns rather than a turret (1667 aircraft); and the B-24M, an improved version of the B-24J (2593 aircraft). Liberators were also used by the RAF in bombing and maritime

Consolidated B-24J Liberator

Powerplant:	four 895kW (1200hp) Pratt & Whitney R-1830-65 radial engines
Performance:	max speed 467km/h (290mph); service ceiling 8535m (28,000ft); range 3220km (2000 miles) with a 3992kg (8800lb) bomb load.
Weights:	empty 16,556kg (36,500lb); maximum take-off 29,484kg (65,000lb)
Dimensions:	wing span 33.53m (110ft); length 20.47m (67ft 2in); height 5.49m (18ft)
Armament:	ten 12.7mm (0.50in) machine guns, plus a normal bomb load of 3992kg (8800lb)

reconnaissance roles, mainly in the Far East in the former case.

A B-24 in flight over the Rocky Mountains.

CONSOLIDATED PBY CATALINA

One of the most famous and familiar aircraft of its day, the PBY Catalina had a distinguished service record in many theatres of war.

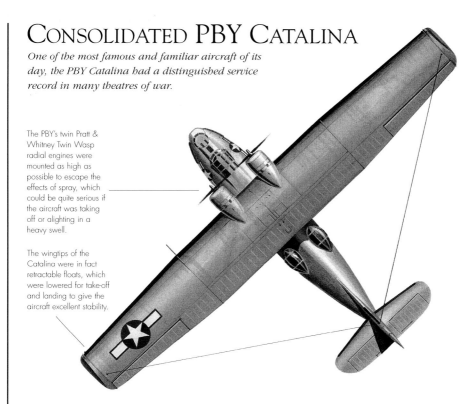

The PBY's twin Pratt & Whitney Twin Wasp radial engines were mounted as high as possible to escape the effects of spray, which could be quite serious if the aircraft was taking off or alighting in a heavy swell.

The wingtips of the Catalina were in fact retractable floats, which were lowered for take-off and landing to give the aircraft excellent stability.

The large observation blisters, first installed in the PBY-4, provided excellent visual coverage. The waist gunners stood on a semi-circular platform, allowing them to traverse their guns over a wide arc.

The bow cabin accommodated one crew member who acted as gunner, observer and bomb aimer.

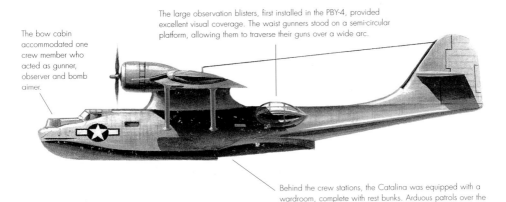

Behind the crew stations, the Catalina was equipped with a wardroom, complete with rest bunks. Arduous patrols over the ocean of 18 hours or more were not unusual.

The prototype PBY Catalina flew for the first time on 21 March 1935, operational deliveries being made to Patrol Squadron VP-11F in October 1936. The initial production version, the PBY-1, was fitted with 634kW (850hp) Pratt & Whitney R-1830-64 engines, and was followed into service in 1937 by 50 PBY-2s, with 746kW

PBY Catalinas based in the Aleutian Islands in the North Pacific.

(1000hp) Pratt & Whitney engines. Three aircraft of the next variant, the PBY-3, were delivered to the USSR in 1938, along with a manufacturing licence. The Soviet version, designated GST and powered by Russian-built 708kW (950hp) M87 engines, was used in the transport role.

AMPHIBIOUS VERSION

The PBY-4, which appeared in 1938, featured the large midships 'blister' observation and gun positions that were to become characteristic of the PBY. Next came the PBY-5, of which 750 were produced, and the PBY-5A, an amphibious version; 794 examples of the latter were produced. The RAF ordered an initial batch of 50 PBYs in 1940 and eventually took delivery of over 650. It was the British who applied the name Catalina to the aircraft, subsequently adopted also by the US Navy. Further development of the Catalina resulted in the PBY-6A (235 aircraft) with revised armament, an enlarged tail and a search radar scanner mounted over the cockpit. Production of the Catalina, which ended in April 1945, included 2398 by Consolidated and 892 by various other manufacturers.

Consolidated PBY Catalina (PBY-5)

Powerplant:	two 895kW (1200hp) Pratt & Whitney R-1830-92 Twin Wasp 14-cylinder radial engines
Performance:	max speed: 306km/h (190mph) at 3200m (10,500ft); cruising speed 288km/h (179mph) at 2135m (7000ft); service ceiling: 4480m (14,700ft); range: 4095km (2545 miles)
Weights:	empty 9485kg (20,910lb); maximum take-off 16,067kg (35,420lb)
Dimensions:	wing span 31.70m (104ft); length: 19.45m (63ft 10.5in); height 6.15m (20ft 2in)
Armament:	four 12.7mm (0.50in) machine guns and one 7.62mm (0.30in) machine gun, plus up to 1814kg (4000lb) of bombs, mines or depth charges, or two torpedoes

UNITED STATES

CURTISS P-40D KITTYHAWK

The Curtiss P-40 Kittyhawk performed excellent service with RAF, RAAF and South African Air Force squadrons of the Desert Air Force, and contributed greatly to the Allies' eventual victory.

The P-40's armament of six 12.7mm (0.50in) machine guns was standard on most American-built fighters of World War II. Each gun was provided with 235 rounds.

Visibility from the cockpit was poor, but adequate for the aircraft's primary role of ground attack. The P-40 was no match for aircraft like the Messerschmitt Bf 109F.

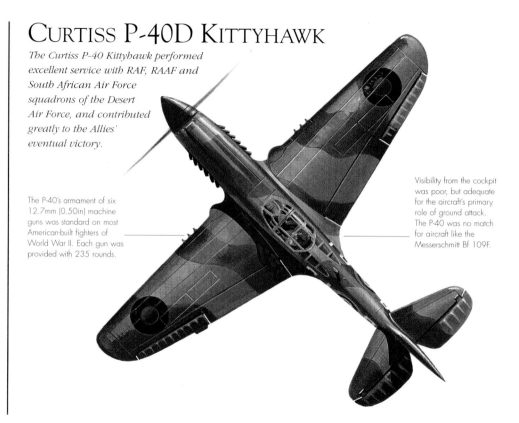

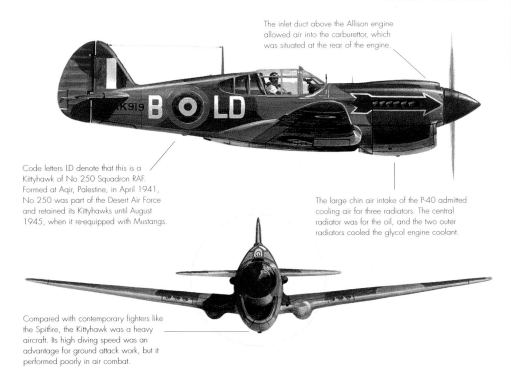

The inlet duct above the Allison engine allowed air into the carburettor, which was situated at the rear of the engine.

Code letters LD denote that this is a Kittyhawk of No 250 Squadron RAF. Formed at Aqir, Palestine, in April 1941, No 250 was part of the Desert Air Force and retained its Kittyhawks until August 1945, when it re-equipped with Mustangs.

The large chin air intake of the P-40 admitted cooling air for three radiators. The central radiator was for the oil, and the two outer radiators cooled the glycol engine coolant.

Compared with contemporary fighters like the Spitfire, the Kittyhawk was a heavy aircraft. Its high diving speed was an advantage for ground attack work, but it performed poorly in air combat.

UNITED STATES

247

Early-model P-40 fighters in the markings of the US Army Air Corps.

Developed from the radial-engined Curtiss P-36A Hawk, the Curtiss XP-40 prototype flew for the first time in October 1938. The US Army Air Corps ordered 524 aircraft, later reduced to 200, and in 1940 the RAF received 140, originally destined for France. Although considered unsuitable for operational use by Fighter Command, the P-40s were fitted with four wing-mounted Browning 7.7mm (0.303in) machine guns and were allocated to Army Co-operation Command as the Tomahawk I, for use in the tactical reconnaissance role.

EXTRA ARMOUR

Aircraft ordered by the USAAC were given extra armour protection and additional armament, and were designated P-40Bs; the RAF received 110 as the Tomahawk IIA. Further P-40 variants were the P-40C, which was fitted with larger, self-sealing fuel tanks and two more wing guns; the P-40D, which was substantially redesigned, its four wing guns being upgraded to 12.7mm (0.50in) calibre and the nose armament removed; the P-40E, with six wing guns; and the Packard Merlin-engined P-40F and P-40L. The P-40N reverted to the Allison. The P-40K was a

Curtiss P-40D Kittyhawk	
Powerplant:	1014kW (1360hp) Allison V-1710-81 V-12 engine
Performance:	maximum speed 609km/h (378mph) at 3200m (10,500ft); service ceiling 11,580m (38,000ft); range 386km (240 miles)
Weights:	empty 2722kg (6000lb); maximum take-off 5171kg (11,400lb)
Dimensions:	wing span 11.38m (37ft 4in); length 10.16m (33ft 4in); height 3.76m (12ft 4in)
Armament:	four 12.7mm (0.50in) machine guns, plus a bomb load of up to three 227kg (500lb) bombs

variant with increased fin area. Total P-40 production (all variants) was 13,738.

P-40Fs taking off from a carrier during Operation Torch, 29 November 1942.

CURTISS SB2C HELLDIVER

Although it had a troubled development phase, the Curtiss SB2C Helldiver went on to become one of the most important weapons in the US Navy's battle against the Japanese.

The Helldiver pictured here is finished in standard US Navy 'midnight blue' upper surfaces and sea-grey under surfaces; paint schemes varied from theatre to theatre.

The SB2C was a low-wing cantilever monoplane largely of metal construction, the outer wing panels folding upward for carrier stowage.

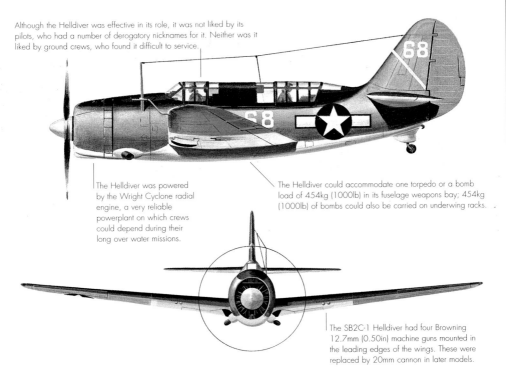

Although the Helldiver was effective in its role, it was not liked by its pilots, who had a number of derogatory nicknames for it. Neither was it liked by ground crews, who found it difficult to service.

The Helldiver was powered by the Wright Cyclone radial engine, a very reliable powerplant on which crews could depend during their long over water missions.

The Helldiver could accommodate one torpedo or a bomb load of 454kg (1000lb) in its fuselage weapons bay; 454kg (1000lb) of bombs could also be carried on underwing racks.

The SB2C-1 Helldiver had four Browning 12.7mm (0.50in) machine guns mounted in the leading edges of the wings. These were replaced by 20mm cannon in later models.

The SB2C Helldiver was designed as a replacement for the SBD Dauntless, which had achieved fame in the Battle of Midway in June 1942. Because of delays caused by the crash of the prototype, the first production Helldiver did not fly until June 1942 and although the aircraft entered service with the US

Curtiss SB2C Helldivers at Naval Air Station Ford Island, Pearl Harbor, towards the end of WWII.

Navy in December 1942, it did not make its operational debut until 11 November 1943, in an attack on the Japanese-held island of Rabaul.

UNPROMISING START

The USAAF took delivery of 900 examples of a ground-attack version, the A-25A, although most were taken over by the US Marine Corps and redesignated SB2C-1A. Despite a rather unpromising start, the Helldiver was of such great value in the Pacific theatre that the US Navy absorbed almost the entire production of over 7000 aircraft. Helldivers were also manufactured in Canada by Fairchild and Canadian Car and Foundry.

Curtiss SB2C-1 Helldiver

Powerplant:	1270kW (1700hp) Wright R-2600-8 Cyclone 14-cylinder radial
Performance:	maximum speed 452km/h (281mph) at 3050m (10,000ft); service ceiling 7375m (24,200ft); range: 2213km (1375 miles)
Weights:	empty 4799kg (10,580lb) maximum take-off 7626kg (16,815lb)
Dimensions:	wing span 15.15m (49ft 8.25in); length 11.18m (36ft 8in); height: 4.00m (13ft 1.5in)
Armament:	four 12.7mm (0.50in) machine guns and two 7.62mm (0.30in) machine guns; bomb load of up to 907kg (2000lb), or one torpedo

A Curtiss SB2C-2 Helldiver in typical Pacific Theatre camouflage.

UNITED STATES

DOUGLAS BOSTON III

*The Douglas Boston attack bomber was used by 18
RAF squadrons in 1942–43, in most cases replacing
the Bristol Blenheim.*

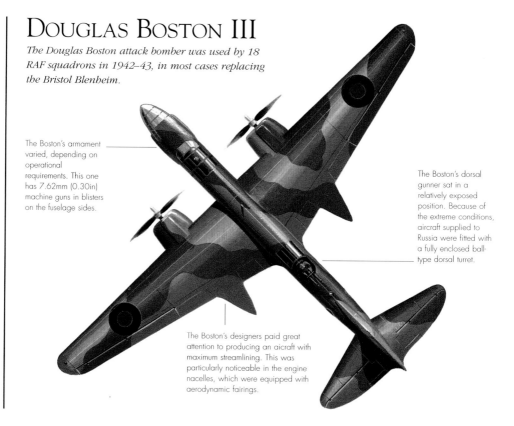

The Boston's armament
varied, depending on
operational
requirements. This one
has 7.62mm (0.30in)
machine guns in blisters
on the fuselage sides.

The Boston's dorsal
gunner sat in a
relatively exposed
position. Because of
the extreme conditions,
aircraft supplied to
Russia were fitted with
a fully enclosed ball-
type dorsal turret.

The Boston's designers paid great
attention to producing an aircraft with
maximum streamlining. This was
particularly noticeable in the engine
nacelles, which were equipped with
aerodynamic fairings.

Although its wartime career was not particularly spectacular, the Boston was popular with its pilots. The cockpit was roomy, with everything in easy reach, and the type was extremely rugged, versatile and dependable.

The insignia carried by this Boston show it to be an aircraft of No 18 Squadron, camouflaged for operations in the Mediterranean theatre. The squadron operated in Italy from October 1943 until the end of the war.

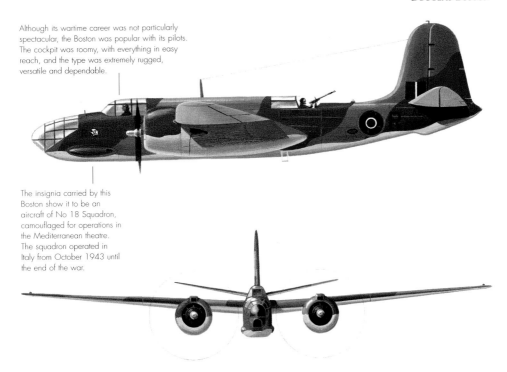

UNITED STATES

255

The Douglas Boston was the Royal Air Force's name for the DB-7 attack bomber, part of a French consignment having been taken over by the RAF after France was overrun in 1940. Designated Boston I and Boston II, these aircraft were respectively used for crew conversion and intruder operations. The first prototype flew

Douglas Boston IIIs of No 88 Squadron, No 2 Group RAF.

on 26 October 1939; 100 examples were ordered by France in February 1940 and 186, designated A-20 and A-20A, by the USAAC three months later. The French order was subsequently increased to 270 DB-7s and 100

DB-7As, the latter having 1193kW (1600hp) Wright Cyclone engines. The RAF ultimately received 781 aircraft, named Boston III, while 808 similar aircraft were produced for the USAAC/USAAF as the A-20C. Of these, 202 went to the RAF as the Boston IIIA. The next major variant was the A-20G, 2850 being built with the 'solid' nose of the fighter variants and an increased bomb-carrying capacity. Later variants were the A-20J (450 built) and A-20K (413), which had a moulded plastic one-piece transparent nose; these were designated Boston IV and V in RAF service.

Douglas A-20G

Powerplant:	two 1270kW (1700hp) Wright R-2600-13 14-cylinder radials
Performance:	maximum speed 546km/h (339mph) at 3050m (10,000ft); service ceiling 7225m (23,700ft); range: 3380km (2100 miles)
Weights:	empty 5534kg (12,200lb); maximum take-off 12,338kg (27,200lb)
Dimensions:	wing span 18.69m (61ft 4in); length 14.63m (47ft 11.33in); height 5.36m (17ft 7in)
Armament: (Boston III)	six 12.7mm (0.50in) machine guns plus bomb load of 1814kg (4000lb)

Total production of the DB-7 series, including the fighter variants, was 7385.

Rows of Bostons and Havocs at the Douglas plant, awaiting delivery.

DOUGLAS C-47 SKYTRAIN

Without question, the transport workhorse of the Allies in World War II was the Douglas C-47, the military version of the immortal DC-3, which had revolutionized commercial air transport in the second half of the 1930s.

The C-47's cabin could accommodate 28 fully equipped troops, or 14 passengers as a sleeper transport/ambulance. The civil DC-3 could carry 21 passengers as standard airliner, or 31 passengers in a high-density configuration.

A principal recognition feature of the C-47 was its wing, which had sharply swept leading edges outboard of the engine nacelles, contrasting sharply with a straight trailing edge.

The C-47 could be fitted out either as a trooper, with folding benches, or as a heavy freighter with a reinforced floor and landing gear and a large cargo-loading door on the port side. The dedicated troop-carrier had the normal DC-3 floor and entry door, and was known as the C-53 Skytrooper.

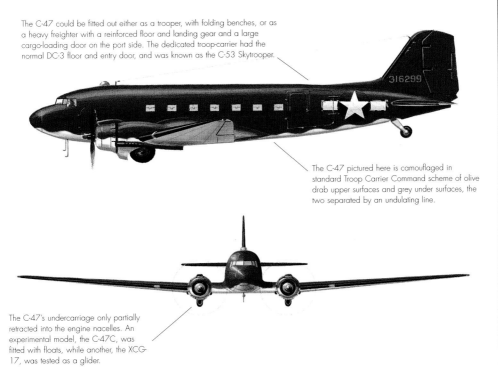

The C-47 pictured here is camouflaged in standard Troop Carrier Command scheme of olive drab upper surfaces and grey under surfaces, the two separated by an undulating line.

The C-47's undercarriage only partially retracted into the engine nacelles. An experimental model, the C-47C, was fitted with floats, while another, the XCG-17, was tested as a glider.

The first of a long line of Douglas commercial transports, the DC-1 appeared in 1932 and was followed by the DC-2, which was an immediate success. The first Douglas commercial transports to be acquired by the US services were a number of DC-2s, designated C-32A and C-34 by the Army

The C-47 was the workhorse of the Allied air transport forces during WWII.

and R2D-1 by the Navy, followed by 35 C-39s; these were hybrids, with DC-2 fuselages and DC-3 tail units and outer wing panels. The first 953 C-47s were troop or cargo transports; these were followed by

4991 C-47As and 3108 C-47Bs, deliveries beginning in 1942.

RENOWNED

More than 1200 C-47s were supplied under Lend-Lease to the RAF, where they were known as the Dakota. Total wartime production of the C-47 series amounted to 10,123 aircraft. In addition, 700 were delivered to the Soviet Union, where a further 2000 examples or so were licence-built as the Lisunov Li-2. The rugged C-47 was renowned in every theatre of war, but it is perhaps best remembered for its part in

Douglas C-47 Skytrain

Powerplant:	two 895kW (1200hp) Pratt & Whitney R-1830-92 14-cylinder radials
Performance:	maximum speed 370km/h (230mph) at 3050m (10,000ft); service ceiling 7315m (24,000ft); range: 2575km (1600 miles)
Weights:	empty 8103kg (17,867lb) maximum take-off 14,061kg (31,000lb)
Dimensions:	wing span 28.90m (95ft); length 19.63m (64ft 5.5in); height 5.20m (17ft 1in)
Armament:	none

the Allied airborne operations in north-west Europe in September 1944.

A C-47 takes off with a Waco CG-4A Hadrian glider in tow.

UNITED STATES

DOUGLAS SBD DAUNTLESS

The Douglas SBD Dauntless was one of the most important aircraft in the US Navy's inventory at the outbreak of the Pacific War, inflicting heavy losses on enemy shipping.

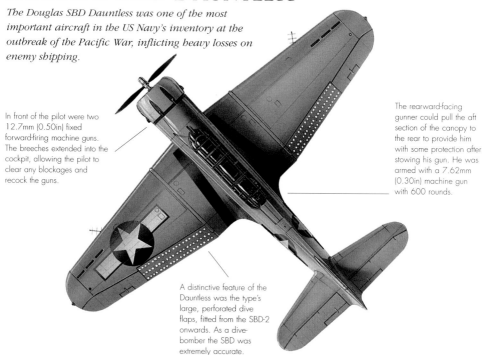

In front of the pilot were two 12.7mm (0.50in) fixed forward-firing machine guns. The breeches extended into the cockpit, allowing the pilot to clear any blockages and recock the guns.

The rearward-facing gunner could pull the aft section of the canopy to the rear to provide him with some protection after stowing his gun. He was armed with a 7.62mm (0.30in) machine gun with 600 rounds.

A distinctive feature of the Dauntless was the type's large, perforated dive flaps, fitted from the SBD-2 onwards. As a dive-bomber the SBD was extremely accurate.

The pilot sat high in the cockpit with an armoured backplate, but no bullet-proof windscreen. A telescopic sight was used for aiming both bombs and guns.

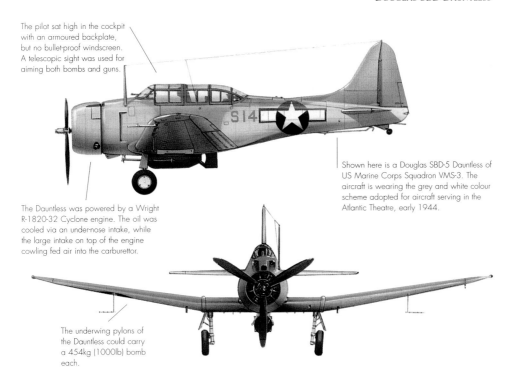

Shown here is a Douglas SBD-5 Dauntless of US Marine Corps Squadron VMS-3. The aircraft is wearing the grey and white colour scheme adopted for aircraft serving in the Atlantic Theatre, early 1944.

The Dauntless was powered by a Wright R-1820-32 Cyclone engine. The oil was cooled via an under-nose intake, while the large intake on top of the engine cowling fed air into the carburettor.

The underwing pylons of the Dauntless could carry a 454kg (1000lb) bomb each.

elivery of the SBD-1 to the US Marine Corps began in mid-1940 and this version was followed by the SBD-2 and SBD-3, with extra fuel tankage, protective armour and autopilot. The Dauntless formed the attack element of the Navy's carrier air groups at the time of the Japanese strike on Pearl Harbor, and the

A trio of Dauntless SBD-3 dive-bombers on a training flight.

type performed extremely well in the great and decisive naval battles of 1942, contributing to the sinking of several Japanese carriers in the Battles of the Coral Sea and Midway.

LOWEST ATTRITION RATE

The attrition rate of the Dauntless squadrons was the lowest of any US carrier aircraft in the Pacific, thanks to the SBD's ability to absorb an amazing amount of battle damage. In October 1942 a new version, the SBD-4, made its appearance. 780 were delivered, fitted with radar and radio-navigation equipment.They were followed by the major production variant, the SBD-5, which had a more powerful 895kW (1200hp) engine. Douglas ended its Dauntless production in July 1944 with the SBD-6, which was fitted

Douglas SBD-5 Dauntless	
Powerplant:	895kW (1200hp) Wright R-1820-60 Cyclone nine-cylinder radial engine
Performance:	Maximum speed 410km/h (255mph); service ceiling: 7780m (25,530ft); range 2519km (1565 miles)
Weights:	empty 2905kg (6406lb); maximum take-off 4853kg (10,700lb)
Dimensions:	wing span 12.66m (41ft 6.5in); length 10.09m (33ft 1.25in); height 4.14m (13ft 7in)
Armament:	two 12.7mm (0.50in) machine guns and two 7.62mm (0.30in) machine guns; external bomb or depth charge load of 1021kg (2250lb)

with a 1007kW (1350hp) R-1820-66 engine. Overall production was 5936 aircraft.

The view from the Dauntless's cockpit was exceptionally good.

GRUMMAN F4F WILDCAT

The Grumman F4F Wildcat, although generally inferior to its principal opponent, the Mitsubishi Zero, fought hard and well in the dark early months of the Pacific War.

The Wildcat is painted in the standard shipboard colour scheme of the early Pacific War years; an unspectacular blue/grey with a light grey underside. From March 1944 US Navy aircraft were finished in a much darker gloss sea-blue finish.

This F4F-4 was flown by Captain Marian E. Carl, the first Marine ace of World War II. Carl served with VMF-223 on Guadalcanal, where the US Marine pilots and their Wildcats achieved everlasting fame. Carl destroyed 16.5 Japanese aircraft while flying Wildcats.

Whereas the F4F-3 had a rather inadequate armament of four Browning 12.7mm (0.50in) machine guns, the F4F-4 carried six. It could also carry two 113kg (250lb) bombs on underwing racks.

The Wildcat's landing gear was robust, designed to withstand the rigours of aircraft carrier operations, where landings were in effect 'controlled crashes'. The undercarriage was retracted manually.

UNITED STATES

The advent of the F4F marked the US Navy's transition from biplane to monoplane, although oddly enough it was developed from a biplane design, the XF4F-1. The first Wildcat prototype designated XF4F-3, flew on 12 February 1939. The first US Navy Wildcats entered service in December 1940, but some

The Wildcat was the standard US Navy fighter until the arrival of the Hellcat.

months earlier the type had already entered service with the Royal Navy as the Martlet, 81 aircraft of a consignment originally intended for France having been taken over.

PEARL HARBOR

In the USA, delivery of the Wildcat was slow, and at the time of the Japanese attack on Pearl Harbor only 183 F4F-3s and 65 F4F-3As were in service with the US Navy and Marine Corps. The principal production Wildcat model, the F4F-4, which featured folding wings, made its appearance in 1941; the prototype flew on 14 April and the variant entered service at the end of the year. Deliveries to the Royal Navy continued, 90 Martlet IIs being followed by 220 Martlet IVs, 312 Mk Vs and 370 Mk VIs. Grumman built 1971 Wildcats up to May 1943, a further 5972 being

Grumman F4F-3 Wildcat

Powerplant:	895kW (1200hp) Pratt & Whitney R-1830-66 radial engine
Performance:	maximum speed 512km/h (318mph) at 5913m (19,400ft); service ceiling 10,638m (34,900ft); range 1239km (770 miles)
Weights:	empty 2471kg (5448lb); maximum take-off 3607kg (7953lb)
Dimensions:	wing span 11.58m (38ft); length 8.76m (28ft 9in); height 3.61m (11ft 10in)
Armament:	six 12.7mm (0.50in) machine guns plus external bomb load up to 91kg (200lb)

produced by Eastern Motors as the FM-1 and FM-2.

The Wildcat displays its tubby contours as its pilot poses for the camera.

GRUMMAN F6F HELLCAT

*In 1943, Japan's formidable Mitsubishi Zero fighter
finally met its match in the shape of the
Grumman F6F Hellcat, the fighter that
won mastery of the Pacific skies for
the Americans.*

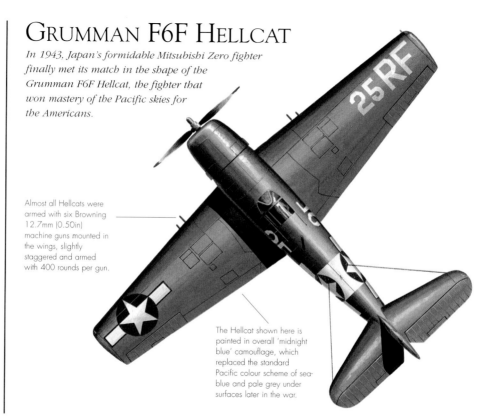

Almost all Hellcats were
armed with six Browning
12.7mm (0.50in)
machine guns mounted in
the wings, slightly
staggered and armed
with 400 rounds per gun.

The Hellcat shown here is
painted in overall 'midnight
blue' camouflage, which
replaced the standard
Pacific colour scheme of sea-
blue and pale grey under
surfaces later in the war.

The pilot sat under a sliding canopy and was well-protected by armour, particularly to the rear. However, no rear-view mirror was provided, and rearward visibility was lacking.

The Hellcat's arrester hook was a 'Sting' unit projecting from the extreme rear of the fuselage. It deployed from a tube mounted in the lower rear fuselage.

The 127mm (5in) rocket was a favoured weapon for ground attack in the later stages of the war. Thousands were expended in the attacks on Iwo Jima and Okinawa. Six could be carried by the Hellcat.

Three auxiliary air intakes under the engine cowling fed cooling air for the engine oil (centre) and supercharger (two side intakes). Cooling gills on the engine cowling could be opened to increase the airflow over the cylinders.

On 30 June 1941 the US Navy placed an order with the Grumman Aircraft Engineering Corporation for a prototype shipboard fighter to be designated XF6F-1. Early combat experience against the Zero fighter led to some important changes being made to the basic concept, and it was as the XF6F-3 that the

An F6F-5 Hellcat tucks in beside the camera ship for a photo call.

definitive prototype was rolled out to make its first flight on 26 June 1942. First deliveries of the Grumman F6F-3 Hellcat, as the fighter was now known, were made to the USS *Essex* on 16 January 1943, and the aircraft saw its first combat over Marcus, one of the Caroline Islands, on 31 August. From the summer of 1943 the replacement of the Wildcat by the Hellcat in the USN's fighter squadrons was rapid, and by the end of the year 2545 F6F-3s had been delivered. Britain received 252 F6F-3s for service with the Fleet Air Arm.

PROMINENT ROLE

In the Pacific the Hellcat played a prominent role in all US naval operations, in particular in the Battle of the Philippine Sea (19/20 June 1944). A more powerful variant, the F6F-5, was fitted with a Pratt & Whitney R-2800-10W engine, capable of developing an emergency power of 1640kW (2200hp) by using water injection. The F6F-5 began to reach the Pacific task forces in the summer of 1944, and 6436 examples of this variant had been built when production ended in November 1945, about one-sixth of the total being F6F-5N night fighters. The Royal Navy

Grumman F6F-5 Hellcat

Powerplant:	1491kW (2000hp) Pratt & Whitney R-2800-10W radial engine
Performance:	maximum speed 612km/h (380mph) at 7132m (23,400ft); service ceiling 11,369m (37,300ft); range 1521km (945 miles)
Weights:	empty 4191kg (9239lb); maximum take-off 7025kg (15,487lb) loaded
Dimensions:	wing span 13.05m (42ft 9.66in); length 10.24m (33ft 7in); height 3.99m (13ft 1in)
Armament:	six 12.7mm (0.50in) machine guns, or two 20mm (0.79in) cannon and four 12.7mm (0.50in) machine guns, plus provision for two 453kg (1000lb) bombs or six 127mm (5in) rockets

took delivery of 930 F6F-5s as Hellcat IIs. In all, 12,272 Hellcats were built.

UNITED STATES

UNITED STATES

GRUMMAN TBF1-C AVENGER

*Although it had a disastrous start to its operational
career at the Battle of Midway in June 1942, when
five out of six aircraft were shot
down in an attack on the
Japanese task force, the
Avenger went on to
become one of the best
shipborne torpedo-
bombers of World War II.*

The Avenger's fuselage was
of oval section and semi-
monocoque construction,
built up from a series of
angle frames and stamped
bulkheads, all covered by a
smooth metal skin.

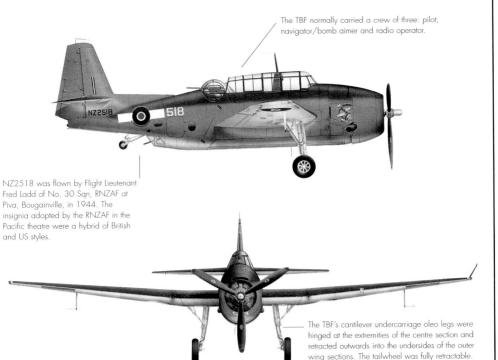

The TBF normally carried a crew of three: pilot, navigator/bomb aimer and radio operator.

NZ2518 was flown by Flight Lieutenant Fred Ladd of No. 30 Sqn, RNZAF at Piva, Bougainville, in 1944. The insignia adopted by the RNZAF in the Pacific theatre were a hybrid of British and US styles.

The TBF's cantilever undercarriage oleo legs were hinged at the extremities of the centre section and retracted outwards into the undersides of the outer wing sections. The tailwheel was fully retractable.

UNITED STATES

The XTBF-1 prototype was first flown on 1 August 1941, an order for 286 aircraft having already been placed. The first production TBF-1 aircraft were delivered to torpedo squadron VT-8 in May 1942, and it was this unit that suffered severe losses at Midway. As well as to Grumman, Avenger production was also

A flight of TBF Avengers approaching its aircraft carrier.

allocated to General Motors, which produced the TBM-1 version.

Sub-variants included the TBF-1C, some of which were fitted with two wing-mounted 20mm (0.79in) cannon, the TBF-1B, which was supplied to the Royal Navy under Lend-Lease and was initially known as the Tarpon, the TBF-1D and TBF-1E with ASV radar, and the TBF-1L with a searchlight in the bomb bay. Production of the TBF-1 and TBM-1, including sub-variants, amounted to 2290 and 2882 aircraft respectively. The Eastern Division of General Motors went on to produce 4664 TBM-3 aircraft with R-2600-20 engines, the sub-variants corresponding with those of the TBF-1s. Britain received 395 TBF-1Bs and 526 TBM-3Bs, and New Zealand 63. Final wartime versions of the Avenger were the camera-equipped TBM-3P and the TBM-3H, with search radar.

Grumman TBF-1C Avenger

Powerplant:	1268kW (1700hp) Wright R-2600-8 Cyclone 14-cylinder radial engine
Performance:	maximum speed 414km/h (257mph) at 3660m (12,000ft); service ceiling 6525m (21,400ft); range 1780km (1105 miles)
Weights:	empty 4788kg (10,555lb); maximum take-off 7876kg (17,364lb)
Dimensions:	wing span 16.51m (54ft 2in); length 12.19m (40ft); height 5.00m (16ft 5in)
Armament:	three 12.7mm (0.50in) machine guns and one 7.62mm (0.30in) machine gun; torpedo, bomb and rocket load up to 1134kg (2500lb)

The Avenger was an excellent torpedo bomber, and contributed greatly to the destruction of Japanese naval power.

UNITED STATES

LOCKHEED HUDSON MK.1

Developed in response to a British requirement for a maritime patrol aircraft, the Lockheed Hudson reached the squadrons of RAF Coastal Command in time to combat the developing U-boat threat.

The glazed nose was occupied by the navigator, who had a seat and a table for his charts. Under his seat was a flat pane window for bomb-aiming.

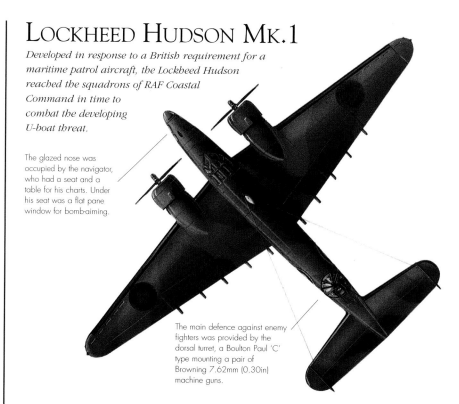

The main defence against enemy fighters was provided by the dorsal turret, a Boulton Paul 'C' type mounting a pair of Browning 7.62mm (0.30in) machine guns.

The Hudson's flight deck contained the pilot and co-pilot, seated side by side. The co-pilot's seat could be folded down to give access to the nose section during flight. The radio operator sat directly behind the pilot.

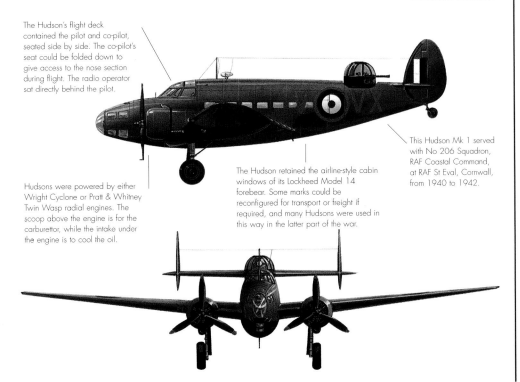

This Hudson Mk 1 served with No 206 Squadron, RAF Coastal Command, at RAF St Eval, Cornwall, from 1940 to 1942.

Hudsons were powered by either Wright Cyclone or Pratt & Whitney Twin Wasp radial engines. The scoop above the engine is for the carburettor, while the intake under the engine is to cool the oil.

The Hudson retained the airline-style cabin windows of its Lockheed Model 14 forebear. Some marks could be reconfigured for transport or freight if required, and many Hudsons were used in this way in the latter part of the war.

UNITED STATES

The Lockheed Hudson maritime patrol aircraft was developed from the Lockheed Model 14 twin-engined commercial airliner. Lockheed supplied 350 Hudson Is and 20 Hudson IIs to the RAF before introducing the Mk III, an improved version of the Mk I with 895kW (1200hp) Wright GR-1820-G205A Cyclone

A Lockheed A-28 Hudson pictured in USAAF colours in early 1942.

engines, ventral and beam gun positions. The RAF received 428 of this version. Further variants supplied to the RAF included 382 Mk IIIAs, 30 Mk IVs, 309 Hudson Vs and 450 Mk VIs.

CLANDESTINE OPERATIONS

In the Far East, Hudsons equipped Nos 1 and 8 Squadrons, RAAF, many of these aircraft being lost in attacks on Japanese forces on the Malay peninsula. The Hudson also served US forces as the A-28 (the Twin Wasp version) and A-28 (the Cylone version). The USAAC took delivery of 82 A-28s and 418 A-29s in 1941–42, 20 A-28s subsequently being transferred to the US Navy as the PBO-1. Hudsons were also used for clandestine operations, ferrying agents to and from France. No 161 (Special Duties) Squadron used several Hudsons in this capacity until

Lockheed Hudson

Powerplant:	two 820kW (1100hp) Wright GR-1820-G102A Cyclone radial engines
Performance:	maximum speed 357km/h (222mph) at sea level; service ceiling 6400m (21,000ft); range 3154km (1960 miles)
Weights:	empty 5817kg (12,825lb); maximum take-off 8845kg (19,500lb)
Dimensions:	wing span 19.96m (65ft 6in); length 13.50m (44ft 3.33in); height 3.32m (10ft 10.5in)
Armament:	seven 7.7mm (0.303in) machine guns plus internal bomb load of 612kg (1350lb).

the end of the war, latterly dropping supplies to agents in Germany itself.

An RAF Coastal Command Hudson, bristling with antennae, guns and rockets.

UNITED STATES

281

LOCKHEED P-38J LIGHTNING

Although it tended to be overshadowed by the Republic P-47 Thunderbolt and the North American P-51 Mustang, the Lockheed P-38 Lightning played a vital part in winning air superiority for the Allies, particularly in the Pacific theatre.

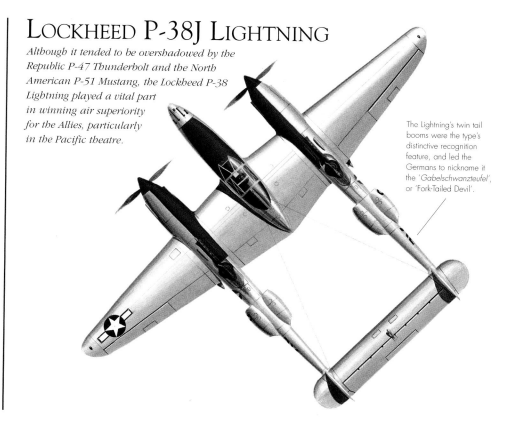

The Lightning's twin tail booms were the type's distinctive recognition feature, and led the Germans to nickname it the *'Gabelschwanzteufel'*, or 'Fork-Tailed Devil'.

From the raised cockpit of the P-38 the pilot had an excellent view forward, unobstructed by a propeller. The canopy hinged backwards and had downward-winding side windows.

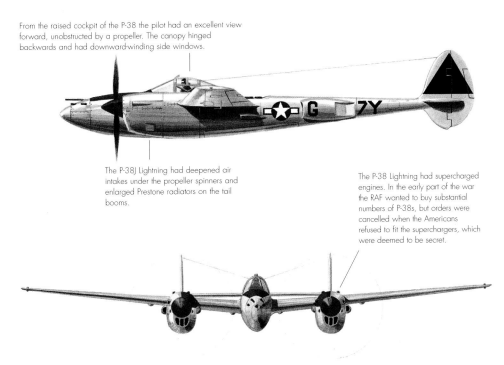

The P-38J Lightning had deepened air intakes under the propeller spinners and enlarged Prestone radiators on the tail booms.

The P-38 Lightning had supercharged engines. In the early part of the war the RAF wanted to buy substantial numbers of P-38s, but orders were cancelled when the Americans refused to fit the superchargers, which were deemed to be secret.

The P-38 was designed to meet a 1937 USAAC specification calling for a high altitude interceptor capable of 580km/h (360mph) at 6100m (20,000ft) and 467km/h (290mph) at sea level. The sole XP-38 prototype flew on 27 January 1939 and was followed by 13 YP-38 evaluation aircraft. An initial production batch of 30

The P-38 Lightning had a powerful nose armament, as this picture shows.

P-38s was built, these being delivered from the summer of 1941; the next production model was the P-38D, 36 of which were produced. In November 1941 the P-38E appeared with more powerful armament

284

but the P-38F, appearing early in 1943, was the first variant to be used in large numbers, operating in Europe from the summer of 1942 and in North Africa from November. 527 were built. This was followed by the P-38G (1082 built) and P-38H (601 built), these variants featuring either armament or engine changes. The largest production quantity was achieved with the P-38L (3923 built), which like the J was equipped with a glazed nose and used as a bomber. The last version was the P-38M, a two-seat variant designed as a night fighter and equipped with radar.

Lockheed P-38J Lightning

Powerplant:	two 1063kW (1425hp) Allison V-1710-91 12-cylinder V-type
Performance:	maximum speed 666km/h (414mph) at 7620m (25,000ft); service ceiling 13,400m (44,000ft); range 3600km (2260 miles)
Weights:	empty 5806kg (12,800lb); maximum take-off 9798kg (21,600lb)
Dimensions:	wing span 11.85m (38ft 10.5in); length 11.53m (37ft 10in); height 2.99m (9ft 10in)
Armament:	one 20mm (0.79in) cannon and four 12.7mm (0.50in) machine guns; external bomb and rocket load of 1814kg (4000lb)

A privately owned P-38 is put through its paces at the Reno Air Show, 1989.

MARTIN B-26 MARAUDER

Although its high landing speed and high wing loading earned it an early reputation as a 'widowmaker', the Martin B-26 proved itself to be a very fine medium bomber as crews gained experience.

The radio room was situated just behind the flight deck. This was considered to be the strongest part of the aircraft, and was designated as the crash station area for the crew. There was an escape hatch in the roof.

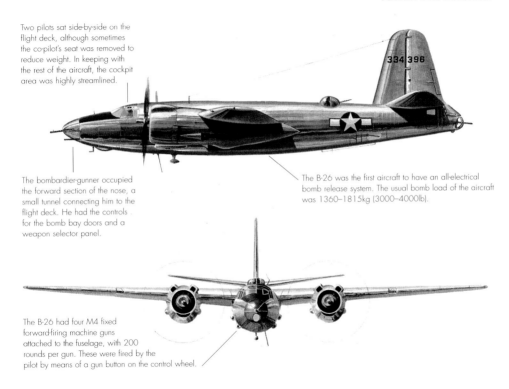

Two pilots sat side-by-side on the flight deck, although sometimes the co-pilot's seat was removed to reduce weight. In keeping with the rest of the aircraft, the cockpit area was highly streamlined.

The bombardier-gunner occupied the forward section of the nose, a small tunnel connecting him to the flight deck. He had the controls for the bomb bay doors and a weapon selector panel.

The B-26 was the first aircraft to have an all-electrical bomb release system. The usual bomb load of the aircraft was 1360–1815kg (3000–4000lb).

The B-26 had four M4 fixed forward-firing machine guns attached to the fuselage, with 200 rounds per gun. These were fired by the pilot by means of a gun button on the control wheel.

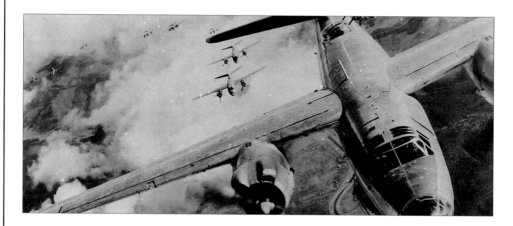

The original design for the B-26 Marauder appeared so impressive that the USAAC ordered 1000 examples before the first flight of the prototype, which took place on 25 November 1940. Deliveries of the first production version, the B-26A, began in 1941, and the aircraft's dangerous flight

B-26 Marauders of the US Ninth Air Force attacking railway yards.

characteristics at once became apparent. After a series of accidents, major modifications were carried out to the design, including an increase in the wing span and an enlargement of the tail surfaces.

In its new guise the aircraft re-emerged in 1942 as the B-26B (1183 built), which had uprated engines, a better armament and increased armour plating for the crew. The B-26B made its operational debut in Europe in May 1943. This variant was followed by 1210 B-26Cs, and 300 B-26Fs with increased wing incidence to improve take-off performance. The final model was the B-26G, 900 of which were completed. The RAF took delivery of 52 B-26As (Marauder Is) and 150 B-26Gs (Marauder IIIs). USAAF Marauders played a prominent part in the crucial Pacific Theatre battles of 1943.

Martin B-26G Marauder

Powerplant:	two 1491kW (2000hp) Pratt & Whitney R-2800-43 Double Wasp radial engines
Performance:	maximum speed 455km/h (283mph) at 1525m (5000ft); service ceiling 6035m (19,800ft); range 1770km (1100 miles)
Weights:	empty 11,476kg (25,300lb); maximum take-off 17,327kg (38,200lb)
Dimensions:	wing span 21.64m (71ft); length 17.09m (56ft 1in); height 6.20m (20ft 4in)
Armament:	eleven 12.7mm (0.50in) machine guns plus bomb load of up to 1814kg (4000lb)

Despite its dangerously high landing speed, the B-26 Marauder was an excellent tactical warplane.

NORTH AMERICAN B-25 MITCHELL

On 16 April 1942, the B-25 Mitchell leapt into the headlines when the aircraft carrier USS Hornet *launched 16 B-25Bs of the 17th AAF Air Group, led by Lt Col J.H. Doolittle, for the first attack on the Japanese homeland.*

Although the B-25C was fitted with uprated R-2600-17 engines, the addition of new combat equipment, especially the dorsal turret, made the variant 61km/h (38mph) slower than earlier B-25s.

The first B-25s to arrive in North Africa were finished in standard USAAF olive drab over neutral grey colours, but these soon faded in the harsh desert conditions and were replaced by the 'desert pink'/azure blue scheme seen here.

The B-25C incorporated changes to the Mitchell found necessary following combat experience with earlier models. These included extra armour, self-sealing fuel tanks and more defensive armament, notably the dorsal gun turret.

The B-25C pictured here belonged to the 487th Bombardment Squadron of the 340th Bombardment Group (Medium), Ninth Air Force, which operated from Sfax, Tunisia, in 1943. The numeral on the tail was the last digit of the aircraft's squadron number, while the letter identified individual aircraft.

UNITED STATES

UNITED STATES

One of the most important US warplanes of World War II, the North American B-25 was designed as a tactical bomber, but found a valuable second role as a potent anti-shipping aircraft in the Pacific Theatre. The prototype flew for the first time in January 1939. The first batch of production B-25s was delivered from

A B-25C Mitchell shows its rugged, businesslike lines.

February 1941, further deliveries comprising 40 B-25As and 120 B-25Bs, the former with self-sealing tanks and the latter with dorsal and ventral turrets but no tail gun position. The B-25C and B-25D were virtually identical.

ANTI-SHIPPING

The dedicated anti-shipping versions of the Mitchell were the B-25G and B-25H, both heavily armed. The next variant, the B-25J, was the most numerous, 4390 being built; it featured either a glazed B-25D nose or, in later aircraft, a 'solid' nose with eight 12.7mm (0.50in) machine guns. In US Navy service the aircraft were used primarily by the US Marine Corps. The Soviet Union also took delivery of 862 Mitchells under Lend-Lease, and substantial numbers were used by the RAF as the Mitchell Mks I-III. Total production of all variants was 9816 aircraft.

North American B-25C Mitchell

Powerplant:	two 1268kW (1700hp) Wright R-2600-13 18-cylinder two-row radial engines
Performance:	maximum speed 457km/h (284mph); service ceiling 6460m (21,200ft); range 2454km (1525 miles) with a 1452kg (3200lb) bomb load
Weights:	empty 9208kg (20,300lb); maximum take-off 18,960kg (41,800lb)
Dimensions:	wing span 20.60m (67ft 7in); length 16.12m (52ft 11in); height 4.82m (15ft 10in)
Armament:	three 12.7mm (0.50in) machine guns, plus an internal and external bomb/torpedo load of 1361kg (3000lb)

These RAF B-25C Mitchells were operated by No 2 Group, Bomber Command.

UNITED STATES

NORTH AMERICAN P-51 MUSTANG

Initially produced in response to a 1940 RAF requirement for a fast, heavily armed fighter able to operate effectively at altitudes in excess of 6100m (20,000ft), the North American P-51 Mustang went on to become one of the most famous fighters of WWII.

By 1944, Mustangs were being delivered unpainted, so that the fighter groups could set to work on their own particular brand of decoration. The 332nd FG employed red tails and red spinners, with red wingtips and code outlines.

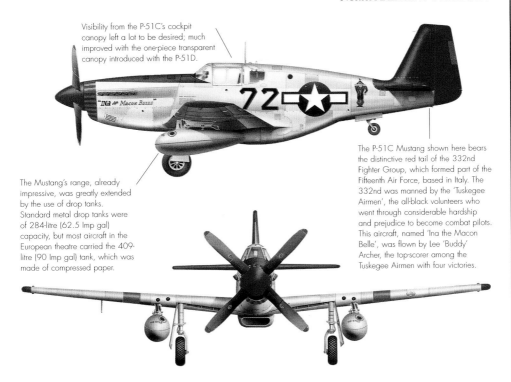

Visibility from the P-51C's cockpit canopy left a lot to be desired; much improved with the one-piece transparent canopy introduced with the P-51D.

The Mustang's range, already impressive, was greatly extended by the use of drop tanks. Standard metal drop tanks were of 284-litre (62.5 Imp gal) capacity, but most aircraft in the European theatre carried the 409-litre (90 Imp gal) tank, which was made of compressed paper.

The P-51C Mustang shown here bears the distinctive red tail of the 332nd Fighter Group, which formed part of the Fifteenth Air Force, based in Italy. The 332nd was manned by the 'Tuskegee Airmen', the all-black volunteers who went through considerable hardship and prejudice to become combat pilots. This aircraft, named 'Ina the Macon Belle', was flown by Lee 'Buddy' Archer, the top-scorer among the Tuskegee Airmen with four victories.

UNITED STATES

UNITED STATES

The first of 320 production Mustang Is for the RAF flew on 1 May 1941, powered by an 820kW (1100hp) Allison V-1710-39 engine. The first two USAAF Mustang variants designated A-36A and P-51A, were also fitted with Allison engines. Trials with Mustangs fitted with Packard-built Rolls-Royce Merlin 61 engines

P-51 Mustangs of the 1st Air Commando over the Chin Hills, Burma.

showed a dramatic improvement in performance, maximum speed being raised from 627km/h (390mph) to 710km/h (441mph), and production of the Merlin-powered P-51B got under way in late 1942.

FIRST MISSION

P-51Bs of the 354th Fighter Group flew their first operational escort mission from England in December 1943. The most numerous Mustang variant was the P-51D, with a one-piece sliding cockpit canopy and a dorsal fin; the first aircraft arrived in England in the late spring of 1944 and quickly became standard equipment for the USAAF Eighth Fighter Command. In the Pacific, Mustangs operating from the captured Japanese islands of Iwo Jima and Okinawa had the task of escorting B-29s to their targets and neutralizing the Japanese air force on the ground. Production

North American P-51C Mustang

Powerplant:	one 1044kW (1400hp) Packard Rolls-Royce Merlin V-1650-3 engine
Performance:	maximum speed 704km/h (437mph) at 7620m (25,000ft); service ceiling 12,770m (41,900ft); range 3540km (2200 miles)
Weights:	empty 3130kg (6840lb); 5080kg (11,200lb) loaded
Dimensions:	wing span 11.28m (37ft 0.25in); length 9.85m (32ft 3.33in); height 3.71m (12ft 2in)
Armament:	six 12.7mm (0.50in) machine guns, plus up to two 454kg (1000lb) bombs or six 12.7cm (5in) rockets

totalled 7956 P-51Ds and 1337 basically similar P-51Ks.

A P-51 Mustang of the 355th Fighter Group, USAAF, pictured in 1944.

UNITED STATES

NORTHROP P-61 BLACK WIDOW

The Northrop P-61 Black Widow was designed from the outset as a night fighter. It scored spectacular successes in the Pacific, where a lack of Allied night fighters had made it relatively safe for Japanese bombers to operate under cover of darkness.

The P-61 had a massive spread of wing, even bigger than that of today's F-15, and a crew area considerably more spacious than most medium bombers.

The radar operator had the best position in the P-61, installed above and behind the pilot with an excellent forward view.

The streamlined four-gun dorsal turret caused aerodynamic buffeting when fitted to the P-61A, but a slight lengthening of the nose in the P-61B cured the problem.

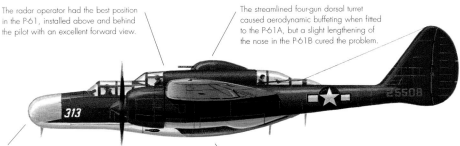

The SCR-720 radar was an advanced piece of equipment, having anti-jamming features which would seek out an enemy aircraft even if the latter were using countermeasures.

Wartime research at MIT discovered that the best camouflage for rendering a night fighter 'invisible' when caught in searchlight beams was found to be a very glossy black, but before this was recommended the first Black Widows were painted in olive drab and neutral grey, like the aircraft seen here.

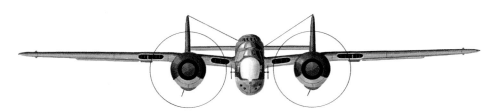

UNITED STATES

The P-61 Black Widow was originally developed in early 1941 for possible service with the RAF, under the designation XP-61, but it was November 1943 before the first production P-61A Black Widow aircraft appeared. The P-61 was fitted with a Westinghouse SCR-270 AI radar, which had a British magnetron. Early

Newly gloss-painted P-61s lined up awaiting delivery to combat units.

P-61A operations were plagued by unserviceability of the aircraft's Pratt & Whitney R-2800-65 engines, and after 200 P-61As had been built production switched to the P-61B, of which 450 were built.

NIGHT INTRUDER

Among other improvements, the P-61B had four underwing hardpoints for the carriage of bombs or drop tanks. The last production version of the Black Widow was the P-61C, which had 2088kW (2800hp) R-2800-73 engines; 41 were built. In the immediate post-war years P-61s were replaced by the North American P-82 Twin Mustang. The P-61 served in all theatres of war, and enjoyed particular success in the Pacific as a night intruder, attacking enemy shipping as well as targets on land.

Northrop P-61B Black Widow

Powerplant:	two 1491kW (2000hp) Pratt & Whitney R-2800-65 18-cylinder radial engines
Performance:	maximum speed 589km/h (366mph) at 6095m (20,000ft); service ceiling 10,090m (33,100ft); range 4506km (2800 miles)
Weights:	empty 10,637kg (23,450lb); maximum take-off 13,472kg (29,700lb)
Dimensions:	wing span 20.12m (66ft); length 15.11m (49ft 7in); height 4.46m (14ft 8in)
Armament:	four 20mm (0.79in) cannon; provision for four 726kg (1600lb) bombs ; four 12.7mm (0.50in) machine guns in dorsal turret

Northrop P-61A 'Double Trouble' over the Pacific. Production switched to the P-61B after 200 P-61As had been built.

PIPER L-4 GRASSHOPPER

The military version of the Piper Cub, the versatile
L-4 Grasshopper saw widespread service in the US
armed forces during World War II and after.

The L-4 was a braced high-wing
monoplane, with steel-tube Vee
bracing struts each side. The wing
was an aluminium structure
covered with fabric, and was
fitted with plain aluminium ailerons
and flaps with fabric covering.
There were no trim tabs.

The Grasshopper had a fully enclosed cockpit, seating two crew members in tandem behind dual controls. There was a large door on the right-hand side, and sliding windows on the left.

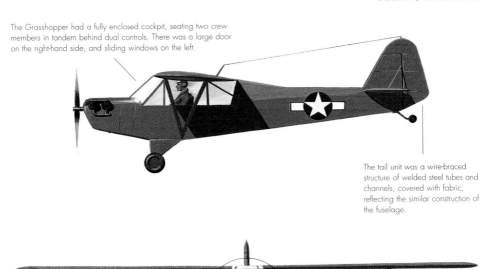

The tail unit was a wire-braced structure of welded steel tubes and channels, covered with fabric, reflecting the similar construction of the fuselage.

The Grasshopper's undercarriage was a fixed tailwheel type, with two side Vees and two half axles hinged to a cabane below the fuselage. The wheeled undercarriage could be replaced by skis or floats.

In 1937, W.T. Piper, former secretary and treasurer of the Taylor Aircraft Company, acquired manufacturing and marketing rights for the Taylor Cub, which had first flown in September 1930. Production of the aircraft continued under the direction of the Piper Aircraft Corporation. The original 37kW (50hp) Continental A40-A4 engine

This preserved Piper L-4 bears its original USAAF colours.

was soon replaced by a 37kW (50hp) A50-4 or A50-5 with dual ignition in the J-3C-50 Cub. The resulting improvement in performance made this already attractive light plane extremely marketable, and 737 were built in the new company's first year of operation. The type became even more popular when the engine was re-rated to produce 48.5kW (65hp).

MILITARY VARIANT

The military variant of the Piper Cub, the L-4 Grasshopper was selected for service in the USAAC in 1941, largely because of its impressive ability to operate from virtually any terrain and in very confined spaces. Over 5500 were built, serving in all theatres of war. The Grasshopper operated in numerous

Piper L-4 Grasshopper

Powerplant:	48.5kW (65hp) Continental O-170-3 4-cylinder air-cooled engine
Performance:	maximum speed 137km/h (85mph); service ceiling 2835m (9300ft); range 402km (250 miles)
Weights:	empty 290kg (640lb); maximum take-off 553kg (1220lb)
Dimensions:	wing span: 10.74m (35ft 3in) length: 6.70m (22ft) height: 2.03m (6ft 8in)
Armament:	none

capacities, including casualty evacuation, resupply of troops in forward areas, liaison and front-line reconnaissance. It remained in service for many years after the war, until the helicopter gradually took over its roles.

The Piper L-4 had a unique ability to operate from rough jungle airstrips.

REPUBLIC YP-47M THUNDERBOLT

One of the truly great fighter aircraft of all time, the Republic P-47 Thunderbolt was built around the most powerful engine then available, the 1491kW (2000hp) Pratt & Whitney Double Wasp radial.

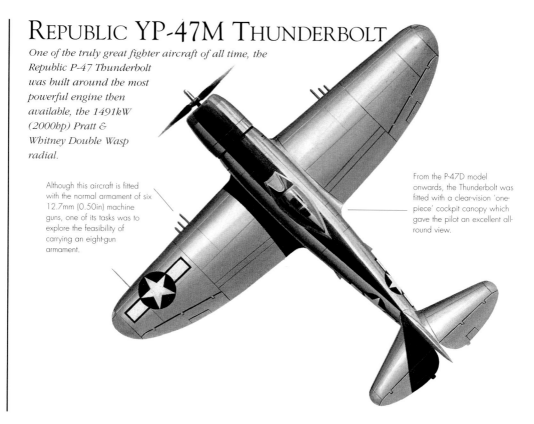

Although this aircraft is fitted with the normal armament of six 12.7mm (0.50in) machine guns, one of its tasks was to explore the feasibility of carrying an eight-gun armament.

From the P-47D model onwards, the Thunderbolt was fitted with a clear-vision 'one-piece' cockpit canopy which gave the pilot an excellent all-round view.

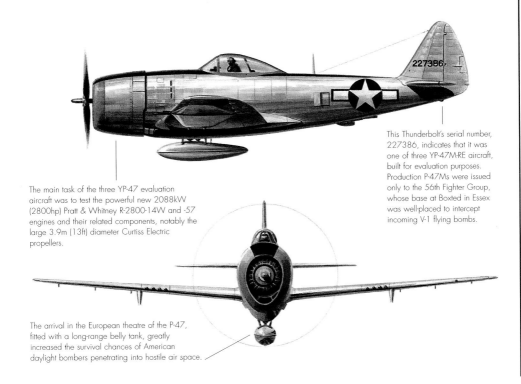

The main task of the three YP-47 evaluation aircraft was to test the powerful new 2088kW (2800hp) Pratt & Whitney R-2800-14W and -57 engines and their related components, notably the large 3.9m (13ft) diameter Curtiss Electric propellers.

This Thunderbolt's serial number, 227386, indicates that it was one of three YP-47M-RE aircraft, built for evaluation purposes. Production P-47Ms were issued only to the 56th Fighter Group, whose base at Boxted in Essex was well-placed to intercept incoming V-1 flying bombs.

The arrival in the European theatre of the P-47, fitted with a long-range belly tank, greatly increased the survival chances of American daylight bombers penetrating into hostile air space.

UNITED STATES

307

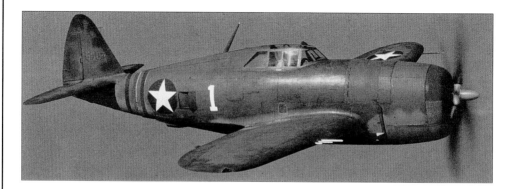

The prototype Thunderbolt, the XB-47B, flew for the first time on 6 May 1941. Aircraft of the initial production version, the P-47B, were issued to the 56th Fighter Group in June 1942. The P-47B was supplanted by the P-47C, which had provision for a belly tank, and the P-47D, which was the major production version. In all, 12,602 P-47Ds were built by Republic in four batches, a further 354

A Republic P-47B Thunderbolt of the 56th Fighter Group in October 1942.

being built by Curtiss-Wright as P-47Gs. The RAF acquired 354 early-model P-47Ds as the Thunderbolt I, and a further 590 later-model P-47Ds were supplied as the Thunderbolt II. The next production version was the P-47M, 130 being completed with the 2088kW (2800hp) R-2800-57 engine. It was built specifically to help combat the V-1 flying bomb attacks on Britain. The last variant was the P-47N, a very long-range escort and fighter bomber, of which Republic built 1816. Overall P-47 production, which ended in December 1945, was 15,660 aircraft. About two-thirds of these, almost all P-47Ds, survived the war and found their way into the air forces of Brazil, Chile, Colombia, Dominica, Ecuador, Mexico, Peru, Turkey and Yugoslavia. France

Republic P-47M Thunderbolt

Powerplant:	2088kW (2800hp) Pratt & Whitney R-2800-57 radial engine
Performance:	maximum speed 761km/h (473mph) at 9145m (30,000ft); service ceiling 12,800m (42,000ft); range 853km (530 miles)
Weights:	empty 4513kg (9950lb); maximum take-off 8800kg (19,400lb)
Dimensions:	wing span 12.43m (40ft 9.5in); length 11.01m (36ft 1.33in); height 4.32m (14ft 2in)
Armament:	six or eight 12.7mm (0.50in) guns

also used the P-47D in its operations against dissidents in Algeria during the 1950s. In WWII the Soviet Union received 195 P-47s out of 203 sent, some were lost en route.

The P-47M Thunderbolt was built to counter the V-1 flying bomb.

VOUGHT F4U CORSAIR

Although tricky to handle as a carrier-based fighter-bomber, the F4U Corsair proved to be one of the superlative combat aircraft of the Pacific war, particularly in the hands of the US Marine Corps.

The Corsair had a nasty stall characteristic of rapidly dropping its port wing, and the pilot needed to be aware of this as the big fighter slowed down to carrier landing speeds.

Early-model Corsairs had limited visibility, with the engine blocking the view over the nose. In later models, the pilot sat in a higher position under a bulged clear-view canopy, and the engine was drooped by 2.5 degrees to improve the pilot's forward vision.

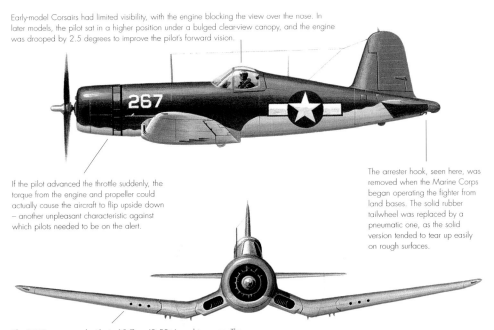

If the pilot advanced the throttle suddenly, the torque from the engine and propeller could actually cause the aircraft to flip upside down – another unpleasant characteristic against which pilots needed to be on the alert.

The arrester hook, seen here, was removed when the Marine Corps began operating the fighter from land bases. The solid rubber tailwheel was replaced by a pneumatic one, as the solid version tended to tear up easily on rough surfaces.

The F4U-1 was armed with six 12.7mm (0.50in) machine guns. The F4U-1C variant was armed with four 20mm (0.79in) cannon, but the Navy preferred the 50-calibre weapons and only 200 F4U-1Cs were built.

UNITED STATES

The prototype XF4U-1 flew for the first time on 29 May 1940, and on 2 April 1941 Vought received a contract for 584 aircraft, to be named Corsair in US Navy service. Because of many essential modifications, however, the first production aircraft did not fly until 25 June 1942. The first F4U-1 was delivered to the

US Marine Corps pilots dash for their Corsairs at a forward base in the Pacific.

USN on 31 July 1944. Carrier trials began in September 1942 and the first Corsair unit, Marine Fighting Squadron VMF-214, was declared combat-ready in December, deploying to Guadalcanal in February 1943.

After trials with VF-12, the Corsair became operational with Navy Fighting Squadron VF-17 in April 1943, deploying to a land base in New Georgia in September.

ROYAL NAVY

Of the 12,681 Corsairs built during WWII, 2012 were supplied to the Royal Navy, equipping 19 squadrons of the Fleet Air Arm; some of these aircraft were diverted to equip three squadrons of the Royal New Zealand Air Force, operating in the Solomons. Variants of the Corsair included the F4U-1C cannon-armed fighter, F4U-1D fighter-bomber, F4U-2

Vought F4U-1 Corsair

Powerplant:	1491kW (2000hp) Pratt & Whitney R-2800-8 radial engine
Performance:	maximum speed 671km/h (417mph) at 6066m (19,900ft); service ceiling 11,247m (36,900ft); range: 1633km (1015 miles)
Weights:	empty 4175kg (9205lb); maximum take-off 6350kg (14,000lb)
Dimensions:	wing span 12.50m (41ft); length 10.17m (33ft 4.5in); height 4.90m (16ft 1in)
Armament:	six 12.7mm (0.50in) machine guns plus up to 907kg (2000lb) of bombs and/or rockets

night fighter, F4U-3 high altitude research version, and F4U-4 fighter.

A US Navy Corsair runs up on the flight deck of a carrier.

UNITED STATES

313

INDEX